Gerald Stanley Lee

The Shadow Christ

An introduction to Christ himself

Gerald Stanley Lee

The Shadow Christ
An introduction to Christ himself

ISBN/EAN: 9783337027971

Printed in Europe, USA, Canada, Australia, Japan

Cover: Foto ©Lupo / pixelio.de

More available books at **www.hansebooks.com**

The Shadow Christ

AN INTRODUCTION TO CHRIST HIMSELF

BY

Gerald Stanley Lee

AUTHOR OF "ABOUT AN OLD NEW ENGLAND CHURCH"

New York
The Century Co.
1899

Contents

PAGE

I THE PAGAN EMPHASIS 1

II THE EMPHASIS OF LIFE 8

III THE EMPHASIS OF THE IDEAL . 12

IV THE HAGAR NATION 19

V THOU SHALT NOT 22

VI THOU SHALT NOT 28

VII THOU SHALT NOT 32

VIII THUS SAITH THE LORD 36

IX MILK AND HONEY 45

X I AM THAT I AM 53

XI THY GENTLENESS HAS MADE ME GREAT 63

XII DEEP CALLETH UNTO DEEP . . 72

XIII WHO GIVETH SONGS IN THE NIGHT 77

XIV WHEN THE PEOPLE SAW THE MOUNTAIN SMOKING THEY STOOD AFAR OFF 83

CONTENTS

XV "WHERE WAST THOU WHEN I LAID THE FOUNDATIONS OF THE EARTH?" 89

XVI CURSE GOD AND DIE 97

XVII DOTH NOT WISDOM CRY AND UNDERSTANDING PUT FORTH HER VOICE? 106

XVIII VANITY! VANITY! ALL IS VANITY 114

XIX THE SHADOW CHRIST 118

XX THE SHADOW CHRIST 123

XXI THE SHADOW CHRIST 128

XXII THE SHADOW CHRIST 134

XXIII THE SHADOW CHRIST 146

A book is the shouting of a man's heart from the housetops.

The public is a cruel confidant. Either it hurts him who dares by not hearing what is most precious to him, for the rumbling of the drays — which is oblivion; or it hurts him when the drivers of the drays shout back — which is fame — the world's rushing compliment of misunderstanding a man instead of ignoring him.

Yet who would not dare?

No man shall lose his soul in risking it with its Larger Self.

Out into the listening darkness, where the shadow audience waits — baffling in its very welcome — this little book goes forth. By far-off lamps it seeks you, by windows never seen; past a mist of faces that an-swer not — and as, one by one, for their little life with the earth-light and your soul, you open these leaves of mine, each brings its greeting from a world I love — its hope and fear of you—before you fold it back into the darkened place, where it shall wait and watch for the coming of men.

A clumsy thing—a little pasteboard and gilding and type—a book—with the hum of the paper-mill lingering in it and the touch of unknowing hands. With the colors of desire and the symbols of experience— to give one's soul to paper—to have it flashed forth in bare black and white, and thrown, like the news of the night, in the dooryards of the world. Paper is but paper to the world, and a book—a book.

But the Great Spirit—who to and fro between our solitudes goes guarding the children of thought—shall read with you these broken memories of days He has walked with me; and Life—the gentle old interpreter—shall bring the meanings home, at last.

In the brotherhood of play and worship and the humor and awe of truth shall we be wayfarers together. This is not an argument, but the breath of a land that is loved, not gaining its way by a logical use of terms — nay, losing it, perhaps, in low music without words — a spirit — a passing light—like a halo on the hills—with no authority but its shining — perhaps — with no importance but its being loved, with no ambition except to be forgotten when Truth is more beautiful than now. Too reverent of the Unknown God and too proud of the spirit of man to settle anything — a book with but one hope which can come to pass— that in being read it may read you ; and with one truth that can always stand—that of being true to itself.

The Shadow Christ

"A man shall be as the shadow of a great rock in a weary land."

The Shadow Christ

✠

I

The Pagan Emphasis

LOOKING at the world with the cosmic vision that has come to us, there is a tendency to limit the moral genius of the Hebrew to a somewhat smaller place than it really occupies in the supreme civilization of the earth. The faint gleams of our own truth on the eastern horizon of thought have come to us, and it is not unnatural to mistake the afterglows of the waning visions of India for a beautiful gray pagan dawn that will soon suffuse the world and enlighten the Christ. When a strange religion floats to us across the seas, like the chant of countless peoples from the mysterious land of legend, with all the charm and theological romance that dream by the sunrise, the tendency on the part of the rarest men — the world-listeners — is to listen to other revelations overmuch, to come to conclusions that should only be reached by the study of the civilizations they have produced.

The man with an international, inter-eon insight — who has the temperament of a Japanese mirror, who sees through to China when he looks at the reflection of American life, or Buddha when he studies the Beatitudes; whose spiritual life, blending Christ and Confucius, the Koran and the Sermon on the Mount, is a world-anthology, with touches of truth from the Veda and the Old Testament, from Rousseau, Thomas à Kempis, Walt Whitman, Plato, Athanasius and Mrs. Besant — is prone to be grotesque with what would otherwise be a very beautiful conception. Being a whole world by himself, a sum-total *sui generis*, he does not quite know how to master it, and fails signally in the very sense of proportion which he has col-

lected himself from everywhere to illustrate
— to a provincial Christendom. His balance fails generally in the direction of his
favorite ignorance. It would not be called
ignorance. It would be called new knowledge; but, from the Tree in the Garden
until now, new knowledge has been but the
showy side of what men did not know.

It is well to listen to Omar Khayyam
singing like an Æolian harp in the desert,
with the winds that blow down from the
stars, but the Astronomer Poet was not
Persia. The Christian religion is not its
deeds. The pagan religion is not its songs.
Our souls are filled with the dreamy voice
of Mozoomdar, and thoughts, like incense,
swing to and fro out of the reverie-land
of the East; but Mozoomdar is not India.
As long as we judge pagan religions by
their ideals and Christianity by its per-
formances, the place we give to the legacy
of the Hebrew race will be far beneath its
importance.

The emphasis of the half-unveiled—the
beautiful endeavor of the spirit to atone, to

eke out its ignorance with kindness — ever overreaches itself. The fairer comparison of civilizations and revelations is not gained by looking down from the words of Christ to their fruits in the government of the western world, but by looking up from the fruits of the East to the fruits of the West, and from the words of Confucius to the words of Christ. Until that far-off day when words and deeds are synonyms this is the first principle of comparison. Each must be compared with its own kind.

The only way for the western idealist to vitally appreciate the Hebrew who made him possible is to be transmigrated from the Browning Club into a sleepy little heathen Hindoo, toddling around a bungalow, wondering what everything is about, until, brought up to dream in the India schools, through the religion and the life of his people he moves out at last to the thought of the world and discovers Christianity.

In comparing the Hebrew and other contributions to humanity, a man born in

a Christian country is at a singular philosophical disadvantage. He has to think
his way backward to the pagan religions,—
almost as confusing and untrue as render-
ing "Parsifal" backward, note by note, or
culminating the great drama of Bayreuth
with the dark wonder of the Kundry motif,
instead of the Saviour strains of the Grail,
and the echoing Glaubenstema. Mozoomdar follows the logical order of revelation. As his heart widens out he thinks
his way — not backward, but forward, over
dead nations and sleeping gods, to the
climax of human faith. His spiritual experience is arranged by sheer circumstance,
according to the dramatic unities. In ex-
pressing philosophically the Christian point
of view he has but to think his life. Canon
Farrar, in trying to realize the pagan point
of view, would have to *un*think his life —
if a word may be coined, the very awk-
wardness of which reveals its meaning.
Our knowledge constitutes our ignorance
of the ethnic religions. The perspectives
are disturbed and the shadows are in the

1*

wrong places, but a pagan approaches Christianity the way the world did. Every man born into the natural heathenism of being a boy follows spiritually the logical order of revelation in his own life; but Chunder Sen, when his soul peers over the utmost of his native worship and gazes for the first time upon the vision of Judea, follows the old heartache of the world, and onward — like a miniature human race moving through his soul — through the faiths of centuries and beautiful dead ideals he passes to his God. It is a cosmic experience. The heartbeat of all the nations shall be in the love of such a man for One who, like Day and Night, shines and shadows over all lands and peoples until they know Him.

His Christianity alone can have the world-depth, to whom has come the wandering through the world to reach it. He thinks centuries, and wonders religions that we can only guess. We can never conceive the climax of the Hebrew revelation. We have not experienced it as a climax. We can

state it — we can write down symbols,
guessed from our unthinking — but we cannot unwind the years that are gone, and we
can hear but faintly in the far-off place of
books the footsteps of our fathers coming
to our faith. With the wistfulness of the
Messiah has come to our Christianity the
emphasis from above, and that which appeals to the converted Hindoo as a climax
is to us an uncompleted prophecy still seeking for its higher self, in the day when our
revelation shall be our civilization, and not
the token of it, and belief shall be life.
But with his actual biography of conviction the converted Hindoo enters into a
religion which is a cosmic symphony, filled
with the struggles and dreams of belief,
retrospective, dark, and splendid with memory, and glad with the Final Word — he
comes with the ethnic emphasis — the emphasis from below.

II

The Emphasis of Life

By taking the centuries one by one into its confidence a great book lives. One year at a time it earns its greatness. It is immortal, because it never lets a moment go. The world shall be filled with no passion or question or despair it will not share. It knocks at every door. It beats down every barrier. With the flush of its mighty youth it gathers its thousand years. It throws itself upon life, the substance of which immortality is made.

A Bible lives because it strives—adapting, resisting, impelling. It lives by being lived. Renewed with each new childhood of the earth, forever in the heyday of its strength — men call it old because it has been young so long.

The assertion that he who knows the
Scriptures will possess all knowledge, made
with the deftly concealed autobiographical
feeling of the man who is obliged to make
it, is founded upon an underestimate of a
book the very first principle of which is
that it is so intimate with life that it cannot be interpreted by itself and requires all
knowledge to show how true it is.   It finds
its authority in seeking out the answer of the
human race.   From the beginning to the
end it seems to search — " Is not this true ? "
A divinely unfinished book, faith does not
consist in repeating it.   Faith is our life
with it.   It does not live for us.   It does
not see for us or see to stop our seeing.
It was not inspired to stop inspiration.   It
will receive before it gives.

The disciples did not follow the Master
because they believed in Him.   They believed in Him because He made them believe in their own lives.   The faith of the
Son of God was His faith in the sons of
men.   Crying His faith upon the very cross,
it is His divinity that he brought out the

divinity of those who crucified Him, that
he had the divine daring to give them divine work to do and divine things to see,
and showed them that they could see and
do them. It is His divinity that He strives
with men, not through a book, but through
a life that completes the book — through
that greater soul, wrapped like a larger
self around every man, which is the diviner
half of the Bible; which, whether it be
called the Christian Consciousness, or the
world, or life, is at once the approach and
the issue of the truth — the eternal, tireless, patient emphasis of God.

But while the pervading human life is
the pathway the Father of the prophets
has placed before His book, no one who
has not a private door shall enter there.
The youth who reads looks forward to his
own soul, and to him who sees his life behind him, the story of Israel is the clumsy,
halting, mimic Bible he has been himself.
Egypt is his metaphor. The wilderness
his figure of speech. The Leviticus period
that comes to all development, the Elijah

attitude, the David time of war and song, the period of Proverbs, of captivity — he has lived but these. The Isaiah spirit seeking him at last and opening the vision of faith, the Bible is God's account of him. Strange, and sad, and beautiful, and helpless, and perverse, he comes to his New Testament as the Hebrews came to theirs. He but reads the Bible with his own.

The omnipresence of the Great Book is but the omnipresence of life. It makes every century the comrade of ours, and every man its parable. The contemporaneous is history flattened out. All time covers every moment like the sea. The world is the huge mimicry of a single man. The great abstractions that govern nations are but the inventories of old histories. Theology is biography. Men are the creed of God.

An empty Bible, in an empty universe, in an empty life,— to him who dares to read a Bible by itself.

III

The Emphasis of the Ideal

BUT between the Hebrew unfolding his
thousand-year vision and the insight of
our modern life has arisen, under the guise
of freedom of thought, a slavery to the
matter-of-fact, a scientific petulance which
has strangely disturbed the real spiritual
values of the Old Testament.

Forgetting in the first importance of a
fact (its being true) its second importance
(its being kept where it belongs), the huge
Moment in which we live is prone to be-
wilder the truth with statistics—to forget
the epic outlines, the sweep, the mighty
movement of that vast conception, when,
thousands of years ago, down the footpath
of the Hebrew soul there came a God to
struggle with the nations of the earth.

He may not have come. He may not have thought of coming. Though it be from the beginning to the end, the romance of a national imagination, the sacred ghost-story of the world, it has become the most literal, the most material reality in the history of men. With every fact and every theory brought forth against it, stripped to the nakedness of a dream, the very dreaming of it is the most consummate achievement, the most dynamic event in human destiny.

If the sea is a lie, to have thought of such a sea involves the greatness of the sea itself. If Isaiah was impracticable—if, as a matter of fact, Jehovah did not attempt to put so much in one man,—it is enough to know, so far as essential truth is concerned, that He could if He would. In the mean time, combining gifts that only the divine heats of a hero's heart or the movement of great events could have blended together, Isaiah stands as an abstract of what a great man will be like when he comes—a shadowing forth of the ideal toward which we strive.

The actual is not the truth. It is the part of the truth that has been attained. The ideal is the truth — the whole truth. The criticism that makes a prophet impossible only makes the dream of such a prophet more wonderful — a prophecy in itself. Facts did not create an ideal. Facts cannot destroy it. Facts destroy but facts. If a man is apparently destroyed by being proved a dream, the dream will make a score of men to take his place. It will call to them, struggle with them, lift them to itself.

Nothing is more real than the ideal. Mountains are made of vapor, and the soil of the ground is as the dust of clouds beside it. Brick and mortar are built upon it. Bronze and steel and gold and silver — the hands of men and the fingers of machines — wait upon it. The sheer material forces swung into its mighty service — the levers with which it lifts this little earth, dictating events, dominating nations, guiding philosophies, placing a strip of sky over every life, whirling the globe to every morning with a hope — the world itself is the massive measure of the spirit, the shadow God casts across time and space in stone and iron and fleeting things, of the dreams of men.

The peculiar coördination of powers gathered into an ideal, a hero, and called his personality, we may dissolve. We may dissolve him into the forces of his time. We may dissolve him into his ancestors. But he is there. As a logical ideal he passes into life. His spirit possesses the world. In analyzing the inspirations of the Pentateuch, in showing the several men that Moses may have been, Moses is not removed. We are but given the genealogy of his greatness. If he might have been, he was; and whether he is a prophet or the prophecy of a prophet, he is a personal actuality in human life, and one with which to live. Proving that he is a group of men cannot destroy him, any more than the slip of a scholar's pen could have created him. If it cannot be said of a man named Moses that he incarnated all of such a spirit once, it can be said that the spirit has become his incarnation,— that the incarnation of the Spirit which Christ reserved as the supreme and mightiest form of His Messiahship, has come through the lives of men to this soul of Sinai, that it has made him one of the dominant personalities in the building of a world. He cannot be ignored as a fact—one kind of fact —and he defies the necessity, the moral helplessness, of being dependent upon another. He is a father of facts, though he be a myth. The margin of the Bible does not hold the fate of its great beliefs in its calculations, and the soul of Moses does not rest upon the skill of experts.

Shakspere would be none the less a personality whether he ever existed or not. If three poets had written the plays we call by his name, they would still represent a colossal individuality—a three-poet-power spirit. Whether He who governs the disposition of forces blended the three actually into one manifold life Himself, or left it to the world and the action of events to do it—makes an interesting and important,

but not fundamental, fact with regard to
the content of his genius. The genius is
here. It is a truth. How he came to be
here is a question of fact.

The great spiritual unities, when once
they have come forth and faced the earth,
when they have been wrought into its
experiences, when they have become the
builders of its facts—have become material
in the most material sense; it is only the
passing phase, the morbid literalness of
our scientific spirit, which could have made
the nobler unities so dependent on the
smaller ones as to imperil faith.

In tracing the evolution of the Christ
idea, there would be a superficial and plau-
sible convenience in arranging chronology
so that Job would come between David
and Isaiah; but, according to the content
of his message and the unities of the truth,
Job furnishes the link between David and
Isaiah, though he prepared his message,
perhaps, in an aloof life, and may have
been singing in one wilderness while Moses
was ruling in another.

2

Indomitably relevant, a great man places himself, like a great truth, where the tyranny of circumstance, the commands of time and place, are beneath his feet. He partakes of the ways of God. In the distinction between the truth, which is the spirit, and the fact, which is the incident of the spirit, lies the only defense of the great Scriptural ideals. Ideals can only be defended by ideals. The facts, though they have incalculable modifying value, did not create the truth. They can neither save nor destroy it.

IV

The Hagar Nation

UPON our unshamed Gentile lips there
shall be no unhallowed criticism of the
saddened prophet-people that walk alone
before the nations of the earth, with the
fire of the old expectancy still beautiful in
their eyes.

Guilty, for hundreds of years, of a per-
secution which is the vastest cowardice of
history; as disgraced men, who have re-
venged with eighteen vindictive centuries
the pitiful blunder of a day,—only in the
utmost humbleness, with the tenderness of
the One we cherish, shall the Gentiles say,
" *Thou* didst crucify Him," or dare accuse
the mightier nation for that one vast, swift
moment, which shall be forever its awful
title to more love and more forgiveness

than all the nations of the earth—because
they took the cross that we would have
had ready, and did our crucifying for us.
The silence of Christ shall descend upon
our brother's head to-day from those who,
in the century when He came, would have
led Him as a lamb to the slaughter in one
year instead of three—who were not beautiful enough among the nations to have His
mother born amongst us, or great enough
to gather the traditions or sing the dreams
that should feed the childhood of a god.

A nation, the inspiration of whose very
sins has furnished the imperative religion,
and compelled the mightiest literature of
the world,—a nation which has given the
most sublime and consummate expression
of repentance in all the unfolding of the
human heart,— never to be forgiven itself,
—at whose feet the peoples of the earth
have learned to sing and learned to pray,—
without whom never would the knowledge
have come to us to condemn them, or the
spirit with which to judge them, or the
Christ with which to be superior to them,

—that the Pharisee might be rehearsed
again.

Suffering under the supreme misfortune
of being chosen of God, of being the most
divinely exposed race, working out in its
glowing public soul the salvation of us all,
dedicating its very sins to humanity (sins
sublimely remembered only because they
were immortally confessed) — the Jewish
nation has been condemned by those
whose sins are not even remembered—
ignobly forgotten; and in a world which
the Jew has made possible, we look about
us but to find that he is held responsible
for his crimes, as if they were peculiar to
himself, while his genius for God has been
appropriated as the universal discovery of
men, by peoples who would not have
known that the crimes were crimes, had
not the Jews in psalms and prophecies
taught the stammering nations what sin
was, until, sinning one more sin, in the
shadow of the Cross, they fled from before
the faces of men, with a confession which
is the gospel of the earth.

2*

there has never been a time in history
when a Jew would not rather have given
up all that he had and all that he was
rather than give up being the son of Abraham and Isaac and Jacob, and beginning
his prayers with the beautiful title for God
that was woven of his fathers' names.

He has kept the commandment without
a " Thou shalt not " in it.   He has always
kept it.   There is nothing he will not do
to keep it—except keeping the other commandments; an exception that he shares
with a world which has learned almost
everything from the poor Jew's sins except
not sinning them—a world which did not
even have the "Thou shalt nots" to sin
against.

Ever since the Bible commenced with
pointing out the fruit that could not be
eaten, prohibition has been the one invitation that the human heart was sure to accept, and the profound failure of the Ten
Commandments in the Jewish nation was
the nine negatives.   The first form of the
Hebrew conception of duty—that is, the

typical human conception of duty—was No. There are promises, but the promises are given to those who will not turn to idols, and those who will not marry the Philistines. The Beatitudes of the Old Testament are " Blessed are the ones who will *not*."

There has never been a people in the wide world who started their national life with so definite an idea of what they were not to do. The Old Testament is as largely a book of prohibitions as the New Testament is of invitations. The prophet preaches " If you do not," and the prevailing tone of the gospel is " If you do "; and with prophets anointed to go from place to place making inspired objections, Jehovah was known by what he would not allow, his servants by what they avoided, and even the positive blessings are the rewards of negations; the evolution of a series of righteous acts thus inevitably becoming in Jewish history the evolution of a series of last resorts. Duty is the Alternative.

And yet the negative tone of the Ten

Commandments was supremely logical. The field of vision was the wrong. There were nine things the children of Israel were doing that they ought not to do. There was one that they had better continue to do. The Commandments addressed themselves to the point.

A negative is but the rudimentary form of a positive, and there is a latent affirmative throughout all the Mosaic tendency. But the Ten Commandments were not negative merely because of the low plane of spiritual life among the people. Moses had commenced his career by saying that he could not be a prophet, and the negative was the instinctive and necessary approach of his spirit to the truth. Fifteen hundred years of Hebrew history are stamped with the individuality of one in whom the love of God was wrought out as an imperious obligation to do other than he would. The austerity of the Decalogue was Moses' sternness toward the tenderness in himself. For not out of a mighty aloofness from sin, but out of a mightier intimacy with its aw-

ful will, had this leader of Israel struggled
to the top of Sinai and under the eaves
of the heavens written the desires of his
heart. Lying at the feet of the Most High,
striking with a burning pen across every
desire the terrible, beautiful " Thou Shalt
Not," he was prophet of the struggle,
prophet of the struggle with himself, writing commandments out of his conquered
sins,—weary commandments,—too spent
with victory to sing, too dread of defeat to
sing—the infinite No, and silence. And
thus as the first and necessary stage of the
divine affirmative, No shall stand—the
eternal symbol of the sublime, unwilling
inspiration of the human heart.

Only the No had been lived, and only
the No could be prophesied.

VI

Thou Shalt Not

II

THE men that Christ addressed needed prohibitions quite as much as the freed slaves at the foot of Sinai. It was the achievement of the spiritual experience called the Old Testament that the Beatitudes did not read as Moses would have made them: "Unblessed are they that mourn not, for they shall not be comforted." "Unblessed are they which hunger and thirst not after righteousness, for they shall not be filled." "Cursed are the unmerciful, for they shall obtain no mercy." When Peter was taking his denials back, and the nails were being driven through his hands, there were no mighty "Thou shalt nots" echoing over the pain he had longed for; nor was there a voice calling to his cross,

" Unblessed are ye when men shall not re-
vile you and persecute you for my sake."

"Simon, Simon, son of Jonas, lovest
thou me?"

In the darkness and the swoon:

"THOU KNOWEST THAT I LOVE THEE."
The boast of a dead face.

But Peter would not have died for the
Decalogue—for nine things he could not
do and one that he must. Jesus did not
say, "If you do not come unto me, all ye
that labor and are heavy laden, I will not
give you rest." The soul had lived beyond
the No, and thus while the Man of Galilee
was wont to tell a man to love his wife,
Moses had been wont to put the case,
"Thou shalt not commit adultery." And
in Exodus, "Love thy neighbor as thyself"
is "Thou shalt not kill," a statement not
only failing to be the best means of teaching the son of Abraham to love his neighbor as himself, but not even the best means
of keeping his neighbor alive.

Without doubt it was one of Bathsheba's
charms that she was Uriah's wife; but

David killed Uriah because Bathsheba was beautiful and the Decalogue was not. If, like the soul of Christ, the sixth commandment could have seemed to love David back, if it could have been positive, if it had been something that could have set his pulses beating and drawn him to itself, it would have saved the murder of Uriah; but the sixth commandment was a Not-something. David had to break it to learn what it was. Like death, it had a hollow voice, and to sin or to die is to pass into the land where it speaks, and learn the concealed affirmative.

The sturdy saints of the Old Testament learned the Commandments by breaking them. Through positive experience God wrought his Great Negations into history, and made the way across crime and penitential psalms to The Great Assertions.

The Old Testament would be the most discouraging book in the world to read without knowing that a new one followed it. The Bible is the evolution of an emphasis; its beauty through all the Mosaic influence being the strenuous and terrible beauty, the sublime consciousness, of the Infinite No, until at last it breaks forth in the most beautiful words that were ever sung—the Infinite Yes—the prophecy of Jesus the Christ. Peter and Paul and John saw afterward. They reaffirmed the affirmed. But Isaiah, singing out of his broken life and his broken nation to the people of the Thou Shalt Not, is the most heroic spirit in the annals of men, because he sounded the victorious affirmative that has become forever the courage and the destiny of human life.

VII

Thou Shalt Not

III

IT is a fundamental criticism upon the Ten Commandments that they could not be chanted; that the Israelites sang about Jehovah and what he had done, but they did not sing about what he had told them to do—and that is why they never did it. It is the eternal symbol of ethics,—the conception of duty that cannot sing must weep until it learns to sing. This is Jewish history.

Nothing could be more characteristic of the Hebrew than the way he left Egypt. He did not know where he was going; he knew from what he must get away, and from the beginning he comes to his morality somewhat as he came to the Red Sea, expecting not only a force to drive him

32

into righteousness, but a miracle to help him through with it. The Ten Commandments could not be more exuberant than the inspired experience of the great Sinai leader, and could not but breathe forth in their very form the sublime unwillingness and the bare victory with which they were wrought out.

The fact that Moses was not allowed to enter the Promised Land is one of the revelations of the Old Testament. He was not a Canaan prophet. He was an out-of-Egypt prophet; and it will always be the indictment of Israel that they were willing to live so many years in the Promised Land upon the inspirations of one who was not allowed to enter it—a primary prophet, inspired with a timely ignorance and a timely truth, whose message it was to tell all men that they must not be what they were, but whose greater message will ever be that prophets must not be what Moses was. And while it is but the charity of the historic sense to place every great soul in the frame of his time, and love him for the

3

long heroic generations that he must have lived beyond his brothers; and while no vaster soul shall ever be held accountable for the degraded ways in which little men have used his inspirations to stop the world; it is but a tribute to him who first took the shoes from off his feet and walked on holy ground before the presence of the Lord, to hold his great name strictly within that beautiful fitness in which God gave it to the world. To the children of the Christ shall Sinai rest forever under the shadow of Nebo, nor may we ever forget that, by the decree of God, the prophet of the wilderness belongs to the Wilderness himself.

Hero of the Eternal No—we can almost see him now, standing on the Moab hills, with the pathos of the shut-out years pressed down upon his mighty spirit, trying to look with shaded eyes through the great cloud doors of heaven upon the land that was the promise of the people that he loved. Brave First Listener — with the old Jehovah voices sounding dim and far, with the ache of those unconquered cities in his heart, turning back to Nebo to lie down with God. The silence folds him — with no children near; the winds, the low-voiced winds, beautiful wanderers from the haunts of men, come gently where he is, and with unseen hands touch the softened commandment face; and the Sunset comes and looks, and the Night, and there is One to watch.

So comes to pass the wonderful never-coming-back that men call death — the lonely death that, like his lonely life, God kept for a beautiful secret to himself.

VIII

Thus Saith the Lord

FIFTEEN hundred years more beautiful than Moses, John of the Jordan wilderness comes to us, the last refinement and the highest development of the Mosaic tendency. Standing in the great assertive moment of history with the most specific and immediate Positive that ever fell from the lips of man, there seems to have gathered in him the residuum of that inspired negative which from the beginning had dominated the Hebrew life.

With all the dreaming and the living that had come between; with the mighty modulations that had been wrought in the voice of Sinai by the great Invitation Singers, and those full-hearted ones whom God had anointed to *expect*, it would be an exag-

geration to say that John, the herald of
Jesus, was a kind of contemporary Moses,
facing God in Galilee as the leader of Sinai
had faced him in the burning bush.   But
it would not be an idle exaggeration, and
has within its doubtful boundaries a certain
capacity to work out a thought for us.   Perhaps it is more the picturesqueness of John's
position in history than John himself, but
whether he is really more illustrative or not,
he certainly is more availably illustrative of
the Old-Testament "Thus saith the Lord"
than the Old Testament itself.   Standing in
high relief against the divine life, he drama-
tizes the commanding ethical conception
of fifteen centuries.   It is placed in him
once and forever, bold and strong beside the
conception of eternity.   With all that exuberant atmosphere of promise that a herald
must always have, John surely had about
him a haunting spirit from far back in
the years, a glorified "THOU SHALT NOT,"
which made him as negative as a herald
could be, and be a herald.

As a method either in ethics or religion,

3*

the lineal descendant of NO is MUST. The
spirit which in the rudimentary stages of
prophecy had caused the law to be stated
in negations is the same spirit which in the
rudimentary stages of the Christian truth
causes the gospel to be stated in obligations.
Obligation was John's way of stating it.

The contrasts that have been contrived
between the law on the one side and the
gospel on the other have long since receded
from our thought, and except as conveniences for the stronger statement of lower
and developing phases of the great paradox, they stand as added symbols of that
trait of finiteness, that whimsical dogmatism,
that must ever be detected, as the years go
on, in the deciduous theology of men.

That God is Love, and that Law is the
way he loves us, and that God is Law, and
that Love is the way he rules us, must be
an assured principle in any Messianic pre-
sentation of the truth.   Until we can separ-
ate God from God or make him superior
to himself, there is but one God and he is
the God of the Law, and Jesus is its mighty

Adjective. The question before all the following saviors of the world is not one of
law or one of gospel, but a question as to
the most inspired statement of the gospel
law. This is the question that John asked
Jesus—" Art thou he that should come, or
look we for another ? "

It was before he had heard of Christ's
evangelistic methods that John had called
him " One the latchet of whose shoes I am
not worthy to unloose." Looking almost
out of his grave to watch himself being
forgotten, the John in the prisoner's cell
was too essentially a preacher not to question the Son of God because he was different from himself. When his disciples returned to him with "Do you not remember,
John, those old sermons of yours, the city
trooping out to meet you — strong men
crying out with a sense of their disobedience—the long lines of weeping penitents
that you baptized in the river ? "—when, as
the shadows grew long in the cell, they told
him the words of Christ, " Come unto me
all ye that labor and are heavy laden and I

will give you rest," there came into the broken old prophet's heart the thought of that greatest sermon of his life and the mighty climax of it, "Who hath warned you to flee from the wrath to come? His fan is in his hand. He will gather his wheat into his garner, but he will burn up the chaff with unquenchable fire." And the more he heard about Jesus, his inscrutable "Abide in me," his eating with publicans, his divine, disreputable love for every one,— the more he wondered how this disastrous tenderness could belong to one in whose face he had seen, one wonderful day, the shining of God.

If Jesus had approached the woman at the well with the air of being better than she was, she would either have doubted it or hated him for it. It was because he offered her the most perfect fellowship at first, and afterward told her all that she ever did, that he was the Son of God.

It is because John would have commenced with the seven husbands and would have conditioned his fellowship, that on hearing the rumors of Jesus he sent word

to him " Art thou he that should come, or
look we for another?" It was the residuum
of the negative. It was the law trying to
state the gospel and the obligation stating
the invitation — a way of reaching men
which Christ himself was never eloquent
enough to attempt — to whom it has ever
belonged to reveal, from the very first, a fellowship divinely unconditioned except by
blindness in men themselves — the distinc-
tive prerogative of whose mighty heart has
ever been the beautiful recklessness with
which he opened it and kept it forever
open.

The law with an open heart is the gospel.
The law with the heart open first.

God may be as frank as he will. It is
the littleness of love that has taught us conditions and economies. The conditions of
fellowship make themselves. The irreverent seeing of too much love, like the seeing
of too many stars, is guarded forever by
blindness. A great heart keeps its secrets
like the sky, by being open.

Though a merely apparent refusal and

but Moses' way of stating his fear to look, the Lord's refusal to let Moses see his face is one of the root-principles of the Decalogue. John was the spiritual descendant of a prophet who would have been ruined at Sinai if he had let the children of Israel become too familiar with him. It was appropriate that he should go out into the wilderness of Jordan to keep his influence. His doctrine depended upon the wilderness, and John was too thorough a theologian to be an immediate convert to one who both by temperament and destiny kept out of it, and mingled with men.

The most characteristic sentence that Jesus ever uttered was " Follow me," and it is because the spirit of the Old Testament says " Go," and the spirit of the New says " Come," that we know that God has been upon the earth.

The emphasis of the Old Testament is in the second person. Its whole attitude is " Thou," and the New Testament which came with Christ is a revealed WE from beginning to end — the mutual book in which the Law lived with the disciples, the terrible "Thus saith the Lord" kneeling down before a few unknowing fishermen to wash their feet. The real distinction between Jesus and his disciples was his incredible approachableness—that he could get nearer to men than men could. The Son of God because he would almost rather have been called the son of man, he abolished forever the Divinity of Distance and made fellowship the supreme attribute of God. With heroic simplicity he risked his mission on the earth, and founded his title to be the ruler of men upon letting them be familiar with him. This is the most sublime and daring adventure in the history of truth. The gospel consisted in knowing him. Redemption consisted in living with him. Salvation, impossible as an act, became inevitable as an acquaintance, and the whole New Testament wins our hearts because our hearts are woven into it. Peter's epistles being published with his denials and Paul's sermons with Christ's — it is a shared book, in which God and men tell how they have loved and judged each other.

Entering into the You and I, beginning to see duty from above, instead of seeing it from below—surrounding it with God —this is knowing what duty is. The opportunity that He and we have together.

The difference between the "Thus saith the Lord" and the "Abide in me" no man has ever told. At once the sublimest and tenderest truth in all the wandering of the human heart—the answer of the wistfulness of thousands of sad dead years—there is nothing beautiful enough to say about it —except silence and living—and living— and living.

IX

Milk and Honey

ON some accounts the best time to have
been a preacher was just before Christ.
Zechariah and Malachi had a great advan-
tage in preaching Jehovah to their congre-
gations. No one could ask for better material for powerful sermons than the minor
prophets had — which explains their being
minor prophets. Their sermons were all
worked out for them. Preaching was sheer
history. The bare facts of the Hebrew
national life were brutally on the side of
the preacher. A Hebrew audience could
almost have been converted with a map;
and spiritual insight, dramatic genius, or
subtlety of philosophy, or ingenuity of
statement would hardly seem to have been
necessary to make a profound impression

upon the Jew. His doctrines had dates and places; his belief was what had happened to him; his convictions were events, and the events said just what the prophets wanted them to.

Wickedness was never remunerative in the Old Testament. The catasfrophes that came upon the wicked were all accurately timed and overwhelmingly convincing. It was a book to delight a preacher's heart — the Arabian Nights of goodness. It had the appeal of appeals to the mass of men. Zechariah and Malachi were fortunate in being preachers just at the end of an Ancient Book, in which everything came out right, and just before the beginning of a New one, in which everything came out divinely and sublimely wrong.

Jehovah began with what his children could understand — with stories — with telling them what he would give them if they would obey him — a new playground called Canaan — milk and honey.

A Bible not full of inventories of property written with a naïve relish that

soothes the guilty human heart, would not
be human enough to have come from God,
or divine enough to have understood humanity; the only difference between the
Jews and the Gentiles in the love of gold
being that the former gained more to love.
David sings, "The Lord is my shepherd;
I shall not want," and the fear of God is
the fear of poverty, and faith is the spiritual interpretation of gold. The Book
of Job, sublime in being an exception, is
founded on the wonder of a righteous man
that the Lord could take away his riches
when he had not sinned. Entering the
presence of the Lord with his teasing, in-
fidel swagger, Satan strikes the keynote
of the Old Testament, "Doth Job serve
God for naught?" — the first anticipation
of Christ's criticism on the origin of the
Jew being curiously made by Satan himself, some fifteen hundred years before.
The Book of Job begins with an imposing
processional of camels, and the woe of it
begins with the fact that the camels are
carried away. It rises by sheer force of

personality into the New-Testament song of suffering, of freedom, of noble defiance of reward and supreme consciousness of God; but all this glowing vision of the soul moves on to the climax, at last, of 1400 sheep and 6000 camels and 1000 yoke of oxen and 1000 she-asses,— the necessary moral to the Jewish mind. Sheep, religion, and camels. Righteousness, milk, and honey. And what the Jews would have done with the Book of Job if it had had a New-Testament ending they told the world with a cross.

Solomon will be wise, but wise enough to be rich. The story of the Queen of Sheba gazing on his glories until "she had no more spirit in her" is handed down from generation to generation of mothers, to teach children morality and the pomp of righteousness; and John himself, writing after Christ and trying to find a figure that would appeal to his people, brings a gold-loving Bible to a close with a shining Hebrew picture of a sapphire heaven, with pavements of the root of evil and pearl gates and jasper walls.

"Blessed are ye when men shall persecute you" was not the text that led the
children of Israel out of Egypt. In the
childhood of religion, their Bible is the
child bible of the human heart. "He that
is greatest among you let him be your ser-
vant" would not have been the watchword
with which Abraham acquired his fortune;
and when Joshua led the people over Jordan, if they could have seen the crosses
with which the King of the Jews rewarded
his disciples, they would have turned back
to Egypt.

Christ's stories to his children ended in
crosses; Moses' in flocks. That a Bible
that had failed to get men to perform their
duties by placing riches at the end of them
should go bravely and divinely on to try
to get them to perform their duties with
crosses at the end of them might seem
strange; but crosses were more practical,
— and Jesus was the Son of God because
he knew it.

Abraham is converted by an offer of
sheep and a nation of grandchildren, and
his Peradventure prayer is one of the great

4

bargaining classics of the world. When Jacob wrestles with the Angel of the Lord, and, getting what he wants, makes it the turning-point of his life and falls forthwith on Esau's neck, and is a good and prosperous saint ever afterwards, it would seem to make the best possible material for teaching ethics. When Joseph, who is the religious lad of the family, is put into a well, only to make the bad brothers bow the knee to him in Egypt; when he resists temptation in Potiphar's house and is forthwith offered the Prime Ministry — nothing could be better, one would think, for impressing the generations with a proper conception of duty than this.

Pharaoh tries to be boldly wicked, and the twelve plagues announce to all men that it does not pay; and when he breaks his word and pursues Israel, his army dwindles down to a few bubbles rising from the bottom of the sea.

Amos and Haggai had all these facts on their side, but they accomplished nothing with them. The Savior of Success failed. The

delicious boyish thrill of Haman's leading
the beggar Mordecai in the king's clothes
around the city, the exultant justice of Haman's hanging on the gallows he had prepared for Mordecai, would make a climax
in a sermon to men; but it failed. In the
New Testament Mordecai would have been
hung, and Jesus, committing the very important mistake of bearing his own cross,
conquers the nations of the earth.

Esther weeping for joy because God rewards her with saving her people, in the
New Testament is Mary weeping in the
darkness under the cry of her child, " My
God, my God, why hast thou forsaken
me ? "

Daniel, made Lord High Chancellor for
saying his prayers under Darius, under
Christ is Peter: " Lord, I am ready to go
with thee both into prison and to death."

The fire comes down from heaven to the
lonely righteousness of Elijah, and he kills
four hundred of Baal's prophets; but we
see Stephen with the dying glory in his
face under the flying stones. No hand

stops them. There was another way. It was to let Paul catch the cross-vision in Stephen's look and bear away the inspiration that was to save the world. The mouths of Daniel's lions are opened in the Coliseum. The flames that would not burn Shadrach break out at the stakes of Christ's disciples, and Nero's torches of Christians flame the light of our sweet and suffering gospel upon the stately walls of Rome.

The foxes have holes and the birds of the air have nests,
But the Son of Man hath not where to lay his head.

The "Thou shalt not" failed. The "Thou shalt" failed. The gospel of bribery failed. They were but the gropings of the human spirit; the wavering intimation of One who said, "I, if I be lifted up, will draw all men unto me."

X

I am that I am

NAAMAN was a foreigner. He did not see any connection between dipping in a particular river seven times and being cured of leprosy. He wondered why five times would not do as well. Cato would have thought the command trivial and unphilosophic. Victor Hugo would have said that Elijah was lacking in a sense of humor, and Benjamin Franklin would have gone down to the river and taken an analysis of the water. But it was different with a Hebrew. He preferred not to know why a thing happened. He could not see the connection between the blowing of trumpets and the falling of the walls of Jericho. So it impressed him.

He would have patronized a God he could understand. Gideon was not troubled because he could not see the logical relation between lapping water with the hands and bravery. Napoleon would have chosen his three hundred men by studying them closely, and Xenophon would have philosophized that the men who lapped with their hands showed more self-control than those who greedily knelt down to drink, and would therefore make the better soldiers. Gideon did as he was told. He probably would not have done it at all if he had been told why.

It was when the sun stood still that the sons of Abraham and Isaac were breathless in their piety and overwhelmed with a sense of the righteousness of Jehovah. Amiel stands under the sky and worships the Creator because the sun moves on, and if the sun were to stand still at ten to-morrow half the Christian world would begin to wonder if God existed, and the other half would for the first time be thoroughly convinced he did, and pray as they never had prayed before.   These are two influences toward deity.

The first Hebrew to be impressed with the orderliness of God was Job; but the more thoughtful the Jew became in his religion, the less hold the religion had upon the masses.   And except with the progressive minority the proverb never had the force of the command.   If the reasons for the Decalogue had been published as an appendix, or scattered suggestively through Leviticus and Deuteronomy, it would have honeycombed the Mosaic law with a pathetic and fatal logicalness.   A god giving a reason would have been plaintive to a Hebrew.   Even men did not have to give reasons — except to their superiors.

They could argue with the Voice, but they did not expect the Voice to argue with them.   Aristotle would have died unknown in Canaan.   A command was the only syllogism that a Hebrew understood. It was because Moses never argued, perhaps, that the Lord selected him.   Aaron's argumentative gift furnished the reasons

for a Golden Calf. The reasoning people
are largely on the wrong side in the earlier
revelation. Pharaoh made out an excellent
case against Moses. Moses had nothing to
say except the ten plagues. Elijah was not
a philosopher. He called down the fire
from heaven; and there is no finer scene in
Elijah's life than when he silently throws
his mantle upon Elisha's shoulders without
trying to convince him of anything. No
one but Elijah could have done it, and he
could not have done it except with an Elisha, who was entitled to be a prophet because with one glance into the splendid,
silent face *he knew a man.*

Balaam was full of reasons. Jonah had
it all thought out why he should not go
to Nineveh; but when the Lord's spirit
returned to him, and he was preaching in
the streets of the city, he told them the
facts. It was later, when at a safe and
righteous distance he was serenely waiting
for the city to be destroyed, that he commenced to argue again, and Jehovah left
him. "Why did not the fire come down

from heaven?" And Jonah soon found
himself in a naïve, prophetic distress that
the Lord would not sweep away forty thousand families in earthquake and lightning,
to finish his argument and prove that he
was right.

It was an essentially matter-of-fact inspiration that held the balance of power in
Hebrew history—one which (outside of
the great prophets) explains every great
popular faith and every great popular
movement from the demand for a literal
king to the cross of the figurative One.
The national inspiration came from the
blending of two facts. One was a command, and the other a miracle.

Right was right because God commanded
it. He did not command it because it was
right, and the Hebrew felt bound to a thousand duties because of the orthodox miracle he always required to help him do
them. The obedience that came in the
gospel because the reasons of heaven are
shared with us, was demanded in Leviticus
because the reasons were not shared; and

the miracle, which is a glorified lack of reason, was the far-off deprecating secret symbol with which the hiding human heart approached its open God.   The great sharing
ideal had not been reached.   It was a slave's
religion.   The moral philosophy of the Hebrew was the Lord's convenience, and the
lash of the Egyptian followed his worship
for a thousand years.

In its first conception being a god is being subject to oneself, and, with all his the-
ocratic traditions, the king was guiltily
nearer to the Hebrew heart than the prophet, because a prophet was subject to a
God and a king was a god — having at least
the divinity of doing as he pleased, except
when an unseen power interfered.   Ahab
was the logical outcome of the Decalogue.
With the idea that righteousness consisted
in not having one's will, the stronger a
man was the more right he had to do
wrong and the more inevitable it was that
the king should be the most wicked man in
Israel.   Disobedience was but dealing with
the Commandments in the same spirit with

which they had been written — a fulfilment
of a choice — an ethical conception on which
one does right for the same reason that he
does wrong — because there is something
stronger than he is — the very brutality of
morals, the religious form of cowardice.

In all the most simple concerns of faith
and conduct, unquestioning obedience is
but a higher form of unquestioning disobedience, still maintaining the rudimentary
and barbaric emphasis of force. Elijah's
argument was not with the nature of his
hearers nor with the nature of God, and
the four hundred dead prophets with
which he brought his mighty service to
a close were but the inevitable outcome
of the doctrine he had been preaching.
The children of Israel went to and fro on
the scene of slaughter, looking logically
down into dead faces for the proofs of the
righteousness of God. The bears that
devoured the mockers of Elisha but put
into bear language the essential elements
of Elisha's ethics. The leprosy of Gehazi
was the argument for the tenth com-

mandment. The sinfulness of adultery
was proved by the throwing of stones,
and the unrighteousness of murder was
established beyond all dispute by another
murder.

A law which found its first appeal in not
giving any reasons could only be reason-
ably enforced by not giving any more reasons. The theory of ethics that was based
on a will could only be carried out by force.
It was the time of the unsharing One —
the One who was God on Mount Sinai because he would not give an account of
Himself, and God on the Cross because
He would.

The life of the Messiah was not a denial
of reason, but a definition of it, being from
the first an exaltation both of its sinceri-
ties and possibilities, and always of its dignity. Intuitive rather than dialectic in his
methods, it was the very nature of his
commands that they were insights and
demanded insights — the seeing of reasons
— to keep them. "I am the light of the
world." The unquestioning obedience that

Moses demanded became in the Christ the great sharing ideal of men — the obedience which questions, and then *commands itself.*

The word Why is one of the keynote words running through His influence on the earth — a word around which he gathered all the tragedy and love and sorrow and faith and hope that made him the Great Experience of the world. In all his exasperating interviews with ignorant men, used as it was from the beginning to the end for cunning and cruelty and scoffs and crosses, one of the great fundamental forms of growth which He informed forever with the inspiration of His life was the question mark. The divinest word in the human heart except Yes, and the only way to Yes,— this Why that followed Jesus — a word the limitations of which can only be known by using it, and the inspiration of which is living in the Mind of God. Perfect obedience can only be the sharing of a command, and through the freedom of many a brave and struggling question entering at last into that divine life which belongs to us and to which we belong — the divinity of which is that it commands its own obedience and obeys its own commands.

"They shall say unto me, 'What is His name?'" "And God said unto Moses, 'I AM THAT I AM.'" A non-committal divinity allowed but a non-committal Decalogue. It was but the time of intimation. Jesus was the frankness of God.

XI

Thy Gentleness Has Made Me Great

A PROPHET is one who infers. He abides
in the divine symbols that concentrate
life. He is spiritual, because instead of
needing a thousand facts for one faith,
he gathers from every fact faiths that are
thousandfold. The unknown wraps its
spirit about every knowledge, and every
experience is the symbol of what he knows
without experience. The souls of events
commune with him before they are born
upon the earth. In the passion of his
thought walk the centuries which hour by
hour and day by day his brothers shall
live bitterly through to know. His spirit
comes, a figure of speech. To understand
him is to be a nation in one's heart. He
is the metaphor of a thousand years.

The world's dullness is its literalness. We know the earth by surveys and the sky we have learned with figures, but the prophecies that God would sing to us— one by one we grimly pace them off. They are trodden in sorrow into the creeds of men. Our religion has been seeing after- ward. The only prophet we fear is His- tory—the Brute of Truth—too actual to argue with, too safe in the past to crucify.

Moses was solitary because he looked forward and David a minstrel of the peo- ple because he sang five hundred years of facts. In the naked might of personal- ity, out of oblivion itself a prophecy can come forth, but hundreds of years must visit the heart for a psalm. It took a great many graves for David to sing, and the wine of countless lives, crushed in sorrow and sparkling with gladness, drop by drop, to make songs like these.

The people had lived. So they could sing. Decalogues may be drawn down from a cloud and delivered on stones in a day, but songs are not made while a bush is

burning, or conceived of smoke and thunder while the people wait. With great
slow chords they come — tremulous out of
the past — with shadow choruses they
come, with dead hands to touch the strings
and old souls for melodies. To prophesy
is to anticipate a new experience; to sing
is to bring back the soul of old ones. God
has two prophets for every truth : Moses
gives the law; David sings its life.

The inspirations that have been founded
in the beginning upon a solitary soul obey-
ing a mountain must be founded now upon
the experience of a nation with itself. It
was a literal nation. It could not take its
songs in advance. Its overtures are all
solos. Note by note, life by life, Song is
taught them. David's is an after-song.
So it is a chorus. He sings facts.

But the experience of the nation is the
accompaniment, the innumerable under-
tone, to which David sings, rather than the
song itself. It affords him the choral ef-
fects, those mighty antiphonals between
the soul of a poet and the voices of his age

5

and people, which alone can make the
song of his life an immortal necessity with
men — a multitudinous truth. But as with
all great singers, the greatest fact, the
greatest experience to David, is himself.

To be a great man is to be greater than
a people, and to be a great singer is more
than to sum up a nation in a rhapsody or
write down its heart in a hymnal. It is to
sing more than the nation sings.

Truth calls to every poet: "Thou shalt
come with me. Through shadow and sun
I will lead thee; with dreams I write upon
thy face, and into thy heart I pour forever
the Melody that dwells with me. It shall be
thou." With the tyranny of truth the poet
goes forth, and Life, Life, like the hand of
God, sweeps across the spirit that he calls his
own, and strokes from out the strings the
strange, unwilling songs that sleep within.
Melody will not let him go. "Yea, though
thou art broken, O poet, and in the silence
and the dark thou wouldst lie, thou shalt
sing! The day shall smite thy chords.
In the night shall beautiful truth break in

upon thy rest." Leading by being led,
ordained from the beginning of the world to
be greater than himself, with irrevocable
beauty each new-born song locks the
poet's old self away. If he be a singer,
song shall sing him into a great poet. If
he be a great poet, song shall sing him into
a prophet — or silence shall be his — or
the muffled way where great songs cease,
and the great but broken voices are led to
the forgetting-place of men.

It came to David to be greater than
himself. And to him who is greater than
himself is God God. Not on Mount Sinai,
nor in the biography of Moses, nor in a
book, nor in a temple, but in himself,
David worshiped. So he was a singer.
So he was a prophet; and the greatest
event that had taken place in Hebrew history was the heart of a shepherd lad — a
heart which was a continual discovery to
itself, from the psalms the sheep knew in
the night dews to those the people chanted
when the king was dead, and the singer
was borne to silence. Through a supreme

achievement with himself — a penitent, ·
beautiful self-respect — a self-assertion as
sweet as the trust of a child, there came
to pass in David the first great revolution
in the Old Testament.   The God who is
a Speaker in the Pentateuch is the Listener
in the Psalms.   The law of the gospel —
" The Lord said unto Moses."   The gospel of the law — the first of the Bethlehem
shepherds singing on the hills a thousand
years away with the daring of love.   " Bow
down Thine ear, O Lord, and hear me, for
I am poor and needy, yet the Lord think-
eth upon me.   Make no tarrying, O my
God."

It would seem as if being a Moses were
one of the helpless instincts of life — the
" Thus saith the Lord."   But David's ask-
ing the Creator to listen to his thoughts
is the mightiest acquirement of the Hebrew spirit, and forever marks with the soul
of the psalmist the most difficult crisis in
the approach to God.

The prophecy of Isaiah was supremely
logical, and had that inspiration of inevita-

bleness which the Great Spirit is wont to give to utterance. The coming of Jesus was the unfolding of the only possible plan. His dying on the cross was the very axiom of his being among men at all. His resurrection was as unavoidable as his life, and for a Church not to have followed His message is as unthinkable as the discouragement of God.

But all these have been the unfoldings, the refinements, the inevitable beliefs that came from this first victorious belief of David's, when, thousands of years ago, with no great ages to tell him the way, with the God of Sinai he walked the hills at night and dared to tell Him all his heart.

With an artlessness that makes him man's immortal child, with the Awful One of the clouded mountain — the Thunder One of Moses — wandering with his hand in His hand, prattling of his tiny life to the Creator of the ends of the earth — to David, little one of God, great among men, was the mightiest, loneliest deadlift of faith, in the conquering of the heavens for the earth.

5*

Belonging to a people who had assumed
that what made authority authority at all
was its being outside of themselves; taught
to look out, David dared to look in, and He
who had appealed to men because He was
a Pillar of Fire, appealed to David because
he was in himself.

The crisis which comes to every religion
and to all art came in Hebrew history
with this first great poet. The eternal
issue faced the shepherd boy — the one
that has faced every singer and every
prophet since. It came to him either to
found his faith upon his experience or
upon his inexperience. Either to base his
inspiration upon not being inspired himself,
and fight for the experience of Moses with
an inspiration of not believing in his own,
or to trust himself as a man's only reverent way of trusting God, and to serve
Moses by being a prophet too.

David looked in. He lived within. He
sang his life. Not a minor poet or a sub-
Mosaic prophet, but, like Isaiah and Job and
Jesus, giving to the world, he gave himself.

One of the great self-assertions of history,
the first radiant, humble GOD AND I—
the egoism of a shepherd boy becomes the
ritual of the human heart and the dignity
of a listening God is conferred upon the
children of men.

XII

Deep Calleth Unto Deep

WHILE it is the power of the egoist that he reveals his life, he reveals no more than his life. David was not Solomon or Isaiah or Job, and he shared God's will more than his mind. The old boy-prayers — the outdoor ones — with the night wind in them, and the sleep of lambs, and the awe of the sky, and the nestling communion of a child, he never outgrew. Even through the sturdier ones, to be sung with the clash of shields and the voices of armies, there is something that steals from these — David is always a shepherd boy when he prays. With the child-beauty he stamps forever the relation of man to God. He stands forth in the wise, unhappy world with a philosophic innocence that has never belonged to so great a man before or since.

But he *lived*—this shepherd boy; a beautiful, revealing, singing thing — to live. He could not but spiritualize the law. Spiritualizing is experiencing, and thus came to pass that supreme crisis of the truth — the letter blossoming into the spirit—the law, objective in Moses, subjective in David — the mightier form of inspiration, the noble necessity of song, the heart of a shepherd, the expression of a world.

And indeed, whatever the self may be, self-revelation from the One in the heavens to the singers on the earth and the men who live the songs, is the creative principle of history. Genius is the conviction of ingenuousness. Prophecy the conviction that heaven listens and the earth waits — the helpless destiny of utterance. The world is not divided into singers and listeners. Because he could not keep still about himself, David became the opportunity of God. His prayers are not cata-

logues of desire, and there is more information than petition in this communion of
the shepherd with The Shepherd.

In the jealous, watchful silence with
which men often walk the revelations of
the world and hide their hearts to listen,
past a thousand beautiful doors are they
doomed to go that would be opened if they
opened theirs.   Though the souls that go
to and fro before Him can never hide a
thought, He listens, not because He needs
to listen, but because it is divine to hear His
children speak; and when David tells his
Maker the quaint human thoughts that fill
our little living here, the prayer is not for
the prayer.   It is not for God, but for
the beautiful returns he sends to open
places.   When the heart has been emptied
He comes.   Only the singer listens.   The
self-expression of man is the self-revelation
of God.   The Incarnation — older than
Jesus — is a habit from the beginning of
the world.   He has come to His sons not
by hiding the human, but by calling the
human forth and shining through it.

It is night. Following silence and shadow and sleep into the camp, David listens to the breathing of ·Saul — the breath of hate when it wakes, of murder and pursuit, a shout across the battle — as innocent now as the lambs asleep in his father's flocks. Destinies come and go across David's face — and psalms.

One blow for a hundred wars?

He hears the old brooks in the hills. "Thy gentleness hath made me great." Standing over Saul to long for him, David saw God in himself, and when the waking came Saul knew at last that David must be king, because he had a king's heart.

The king in the gate, peering across the plain — Absalom fighting for the throne — the messengers running — a question — a complete theology. "Is the young man Absalom safe?"

Once he lay with his head on his arm — this shepherd boy, — and he watched the wandering flocks trooping above his sheep. "He would be a king; he would have princes for his sons."

He had not thought of this.

Through the heart-aches of a thousand years the Father-cry—the father-cry, "O my son Absalom, my son, my son Absalom! Would God I had died for thee. O Absalom, my son, my son!"

The king's cry in the gate. The hailing of the Cross. The Fatherhood of God.

XIII

Who Giveth Songs in the Night

ONE would know that David must have
lain awake with these songs of his. The
beautiful broken sleep of a Hebrew king
floats down its music, and for thousands of
years we sing, because David shared the
shadow of the sun with the shining ones,
and in their wakefulness remembered not
his rest.

O listening Night, when the children of
mothers are born, and the children of the
sky come forth, and the songs of the heart,
and the Morning makes ready for Joy.

O watching Night, when souls are un-
locked with the dark and Silence sojourns
with men, when the wind goes forth a
muffled footstep of the day, and Sleep —
from down his eternal ways — Sleep has

come to us, and Dream — the walking of God through sleep!

O Eternal Night, O Infinite Face, bend low. The sun has wandered down the west. The tiny day has gone. Say thou again "Thou belongest unto Me! I am Death. I am Life. I am God. Thou belongest unto Me!"

O Infinite Face, with the shadow I know not of and the light I cannot know, with the shadow I know, I come, with the shadow of earth I come, with David's prayer I come. "Bow down Thine ear, O Lord, for I am poor and needy, yet Thou thinkest upon me. Make no tarrying, O my God."

No one would care what David did after reading these psalms. Hamlet saw the king praying. If he had heard him, he would have forgiven him. Shakspere knew the manner of men too well to let the penitent words be known. It would make a god a God to listen one day to the world, and a man could hardly overhear the human heart for a thousand years without a

divine love in him. It has been wondered
that God could come down to the earth.
He could not help coming. There was a
cross because he had listened to David's
prayers.

It is insolent to wonder that he loves us.
Any one would be a god who knew what
a god knows. The one attribute of God is
omniscience, and his virtues are the necessities of His knowledge. Rising into penitence, forgiveness, and peace, with no
cross to make him bold, even David could
chant in the night watches, " He delivered
me because he delighted in me," and " I
was shapen in iniquity and in sin did my
mother conceive me." The transfiguration
of Moses which the disciples thought they
saw had happened a thousand years before. It was the Singer in the night.

The psalms are the real revelation of the
Decalogue. What Moses stated, David
sang. Commands had become prayers.
It was the limitation of Moses that he sang
but twice, that his song was separated from
everything else. " I will sing unto the

Lord, for He hath triumphed gloriously."
The Ten Commandments were delivered to
a silent people by a silent man. Miriam's
song was not there. There were no re-
sponses. The voices of men sang not
back to God at the foot of Sinai. Singing
had been confined to the Red Sea, but
the Red Sea song, broken loose in David,
sweeps the worship of Israel in his " Praise
ye the Lord " to the very foot of the Commandment mountain, and the laws of Moses are choruses at last, on the lips of the
congregation. The inside of the Ten Commandments came with one who saw them
from the inside. David was the discoverer
of the law's heart. His way of conceiving
duty was praise. His method of doing it
was communion. He has not a song that
does not pray, or a prayer that does
not sing. This was a new thing in the
world. It was a poet's inevitable interpretation of command, gained as a poet
must ever gain his interpretation, through
life itself. He sang his experience of The
Will. It was " Thy gentleness has made
me great."

Jesus was the Redeemer of the Old Testament. He saved it for us. David was the redeemer of Moses. The nobler sense of relatedness, which is the essence of the poetic temperament, gave to the world in him two mighty moods that never had been blended before. Saul loved to listen because it was king's music. The same fingers that found the gentle reveries of the immortal harp held up the head of Goliath before the shouts of soldiers.

Before the darkness of a dream — beautiful dips of the harp which seem to glide down and down and down into the old, old melody that deep below life God keeps for the nearer ones — the melody that seems to sing about music that it came from — not yet for us. Achilles is Homer.

Along the streets the women singing and dancing with tabrets, with joy and with instruments of music, Homer is his own Achilles.

An inspiration of paradox — a soul which is the most intimate revelation between the " I AM " and " He that hath seen Me hath seen the Father." With

6

"sons of Abraham," "sons of Isaac," "sons of Jacob," children of Israel, there is one name folded away with the pillar of cloud. There should never be the title "The son of Moses." Though with a David-place in his heart, it was not for his people to know. The name of God should be "The Son of David."

While it was somewhat to be Homer and Achilles, both at once, it was the greatness of the psalmist that he made men love him. He was the Old Testament atonement — this warrior minstrel — this king-poet, the singer of command, writing the Pentateuch over into hymns, saying his prayers with the Ten Commandments.

XIV

When the People Saw the Mountain Smoking They Stood Afar Off

THE second commandment was against
idols, and the only alternative for the Hebrew was to make an idol of the thick darkness from which the commandment was
issued. This is what he did. The smoke-
god was the ghost of idol worship. The
Voice was in the darkness, and it was care-
fully called the sign of God's presence, and
not God himself. But when the average
Hebrew looked up from his manna-gather-
ing to the pillar in the sky, it was God. It
was exactly God.

The cloud was the first clumsy and yet
beautiful groping of the human heart toward infinity. It was a mystery idol,
carved by the soft airs of heaven. There

were no poor trivial human outlines. It was the idol of the Breath of God, half of heaven and half of the earth, floating over the lives of men like a thought. Always to be glorious because it first caught God away from the stone-loving, material ways of the human heart, a cloud is yet but a cloud, a poor tiny wraith of infinity, tucked over a little mountain way, down under the worlds, on a little earth. The worlds shone on unrecognized.

The essential thing about the pillar of fire was its nearness. It protected the Hebrews from the lonely stars, from the infinity of their God. Children crying in the dark, Jehovah kept a dim light burning over them to show that he was there. They did not know that the night was God.

And yet the very fear of Jehovah had a certain familiarity in it, the sense of a right to constant attention, to striking miracles. There is an impression of a certain haughty intimacy, a divine neighborliness on the part of the One of Sinai that no amount of thunder and lightning and darkness and

terror can quite remove from the early Hebrew thought. An air of close and mutual watchfulness — at once the source of
the moral energy and the philosophical
childishness of the Hebrew — runs through
all the earlier chapters of the Bible, as if
Jehovah were experimenting with the human nature he had made, and men were
experimenting with him.

There is a freshness of atmosphere as if
nothing had ever been done before, as if
the responsibility of sinning the first fresh
sins in all the world came then, with the
glow and zest not left to us, in these later
days, when the iron monotony of evil has
pressed down its awful commonplace upon
the human heart, and we sin too wisely to
sin well — too thoughtfully, with a haunting of an inherited sadness and all the in-
convenient convictions that reflect the experience of men.

Living when all the sins of which we can
think have been used over and over again —
when original sin is called original because
it is not — we look back in the earlier

6*

Scriptures to a time when the originality
of a sin was the most fascinating part of it.

The activity of Jehovah in the Pentateuch, the bustle of morality called forth
by this creative period of immorality, is
noticeably lessened when the sin of Israel
has become a mere inheritance in the land
of Canaan and the uniqueness of disobedience has lost its bloom. God and man
are connected in every verse. Everything
is either right or wrong. Every word
moralizes. In Chronicles, and through the
bad Kings, revelation grows aloof, and
the emphasis of prophecy is changed to
the story of events, as if Jehovah were letting men wander as they would — weary
of history, waiting for something worth
while, or a man to be born like David who
would call out His waiting love and turn
Him toward men again — for their beautiful dreams of what they would be if they
could. There was a time of divine retreat
when the soul of the fathers worshiping
their less familiar God drew closer to Him
in the silence. He had been jealous before

Restive — He had seemed to change His mind, to lose His patience — a new God only beginning to learn how discouraging people were. Through all these cruder days the conception which emphasized His nearness belittled it, and He seems to have taken the opportunity — Infinite God — Incognito — to disguise Himself for the little awe of men in the tawdry passions that they had themselves, before they knew who He was.

The metaphor of a profound philosophy to us, Genesis was not a metaphor to the Hebrew, and this barbaric literalness of God's being almost in the next room was the token both of inspiration and limitation. The Hebrew revelation was inspired enough to begin at the beginning of the mind as well as the beginning of the world; and although it has been a supposed duty to maintain a special private psychology for the Bible — to believe that it could not have been inspired unless it commenced in the middle, or commenced at both ends, or did not commence at all,— the idea of truth looking down on itself as it winds high and higher through its pages, has gained momentum enough to make us distinctly worship God for what the children in the wilderness did not see.

They did not see infinity. The God of their duties was not the Infinite God. Though the Book of Job may have been a poem before the death of Moses, it was certainly not history until after David. Full of the trivial-terrible, Jehovah was a more earnest play-god in the groping childhood of the human spirit.

Before the telescope and the Sermon on the Mount, the compass and the thirteenth of Corinthians had wrought their vast and mutual prophecy; before Paul and Luther and Galileo and Columbus and — Jesus, had unfolded the works and the thoughts of God; under the serene satire of the heavens in the little land of Uz, "Where wast thou when I laid the foundations of the earth,"—Job became the discoverer of infinity.

XV

"Where Wast Thou When I Laid the Foundations of the Earth?"

BUT Job was more than the discoverer of infinity. He was the first to see the bearing of infinity on righteousness. He was the Moses of the sky and the earth and the sea. He connected the Ten Commandments with the universe. He did for the first chapter of Genesis what David did for the twentieth chapter of Exodus. He set it to music. He made it an incentive to action.

The imagination of Job was the science of his day. He turned men to God through the natural world. It was the return of religion to nature, the renaissance of creation. His heart had the further listening in it. He heard the voice beyond the Sinai voice — the Voice of the voice — when darkness was upon the face of the deep, and God out of the infinite shadow moved forth over the chaos of the earth, and the young thunders called across the new seas, and the "morning stars sang together, and all the sons of God shouted for joy."

The Jewish law had not seemed, for the most part, to go back of Mount Sinai. The voice of God was an inland voice; like the voice of man, it had a place where it belonged — the cloud and darkness over a mountain in the wilderness. It was trivial with geography. It was provincial, personal. "The Lord said unto Moses." To bring the Voice out of a desert in Arabia, to teach the world to listen to the silence of the sky and the whisper of the earth — this is the destiny of Job. He looked beyond the Burning Bush. The Day was a Face that watched the lives of men. The Night was a shadow for the sleep of the world.

The prelude to the Ten Commandments had been simply "I am the Lord thy God,

who brought thee out of the land of Egypt."
Egypt was enough infinity for the earlier
Hebrew theology. Mosaic law was based
upon an experience. The great point of
the Hebrew was the Lord's relation to *him*.
He did not care what God had been doing before. Howsoever it may have been,
the earth had been created. Religion was
the sublimer way of getting as much as
possible out of it. The Lord's relation to
others was irrelevant. The Hebrews did
not attempt to make converts of the Egyp-
tians. They took their jewels. Their way
of converting the inhabitants of Canaan
had been to destroy them, and their indifference as to God's relation to other men
took the kindred form of an indifference as
to God's relation to the natural world.
Creation was irrelevant. It had occurred,
and had no practical bearing upon what God
would do next. The natural world was not
an expression of Him, but something that
he had power over, and as long as they were
supplied with manna, and the power was
used in their behalf, they were satisfied.

Abraham was told that his children would
be as the stars for multitude, which statement, instead of being a revelation of creation to Abraham, was a calculation.   He
argued that Jehovah would keep his promise because he had kept other promises.
Job would have argued that the Lord
would keep his promise because he was the
Lord of the stars and promises together.
Job was a poet.   He established a new
connection.

The early Hebrews do not seem to have
been interested in the Lord — as a Lord.
They were too shrewd with Jehovah to
understand Him.   They never forgot themselves.   They approached Him for a pur-
pose, and to the piety that is a mere deifi-
cation of a contract, the Spirit is slow in
revealing itself.   Though dim suggestions
and beautiful outlooks cannot be crowded
out of practical things, in divine revelation,
as in human art, the practical emphasis is
not practical.   The too eager hand belongs
to closed eyes.   We cannot know Dante
by his account-book, nor Shakspere by

his bargains with the actors, and Xantippe never knew Socrates, because she could never see him without compelling him to do something for her.

The point of the Jewish character, which involves almost every failing, from the lie of Abraham to the rejection of Christ, is the characteristic Hebrew inability to see anything in an impersonal way, from God in the heavens to thirty pieces of silver in the hands of a priest. Jacob, wrestling with the angel of the Lord, is the type of Hebrew prayer — blind, splendid, indomitable desire. The blessing is the God. The blessing is what God is for. It is the sublimity of Job that his conception of duty was based not upon what God had done for him, but upon God considered as a God,—the wonder that he would do anything for him at all. The sublimest personal faith in the Old Testament was based upon impersonality itself. For the very reason that God mocked him in the whirlwind, " Where wast thou when I laid the foundations of the earth ? " Job clung

to Him.   It is the mightier faith that is conquered from despair.   The peace of awe was
upon him — the breath from the worlds.
The skepticism of Omar Khayyam was the
faith of Job.   The worship of vastness in
which the Persian felt it logical to lose his
soul, was Job's way of finding his.

" Impotent pieces of the game he plays
Upon this checkerboard of Nights and Days ;
Hither and thither moves and checks and slays,
And one by one in the closet lays.

" And that inverted bowl they call the sky,
Whereunder, crawling, cooped we live and die,
Lift not your hands to It for help — for it
As impotently rolls as you or I."

Another voice :

" Hast thou commanded the morning since thy
        days begun ?
And caused the dayspring to know its place ?—
Hast thou comprehended the breadth of the
        earth ?
Declare if thou knowest it all.
Where is the way to the dwelling of light ?
And as for darkness, where is the place thereof,

That thou shouldst take it to the bound thereof,
And that thou shouldst discern the paths to the
   house thereof?
By what way is the light parted —
Or the east wind scattered upon the earth?
Canst thou send forth lightnings that they may go
And say unto thee, 'Here we are'?"

Singing under Omar Khayyam's sky:

" Oh, that my words were written!
Oh, that they were printed in a book!
That they were graven with an iron pen and lead,
They were graven on the rock forever!
I KNOW THAT MY REDEEMER LIVETH
And that He shall stand at last upon the earth,
And tho' after my skin, worms destroy this body,
Yet in my flesh I shall see God,
Whom I shall see for myself —
And mine eyes shall behold and not another!"

— the angels of the Resurrection fifteen
hundred years away.

   And this is Job, finding glory in being
forgotten. With the night-light his soul
discovered God. Under the hush thereof

" Behold, I am vile.
   I lay mine hand upon my mouth."

" I had heard of Thee by the hearing of the ear,
But now mine eye seeth Thee."

And Job, the inspirer of pain, the redeemer
of sorrow, forging out of despair his mighty
creed, marks the transition from the childhood to the manhood of faith.

The whole human spirit struggles in this
far-off song. The centuries met one night
in this grand old heart. Under the empty
sky they cried themselves out — silenced —
sky-silenced — as long as the spirit of Job
keeps answering in the world. For the
few short years we sojourn under the stars
a song shall follow them. It is Job's sky —
and God's.

The discoverer of a lost Creator, Job was
the first pure, disinterested worshiper that
God ever had. No longer a divine Convenience, a Promise-Divinity, the Creator
was rediscovered — drawn out from the tiny
nook of faith that the desires of men had
made for him, into His Own House.

XVI

Curse God and Die

THE very essence of Job's faith was its breadth. Breadth was its practicalness. The faith of Eliphaz and Zophar and Bildad was too narrow to cover the case. Job cries, "Have pity on me, O my friends. The hand of God hath touched me." Zophar soothes him: "Such is the portion of the wicked man. Terrors come upon him and the heritage decreed from the Mighty One."

Job had lost his children. He had lost his flocks. He had lost all for whom he lived, and he had boils and—friends.

Comforting a poor man in sorrow by telling him that he deserved it, and that he will have more if he does not grant that he deserves it, may seem satirical to the modern mind, but it must be remembered of the friends of Job that they not only began well, by sitting with him seven days and nights and not saying anything, but they offered the very best comfort, when they felt it dutiful to speak, that theology afforded at that time.

Trained to believe that righteousness was remunerative and that unrighteousness was not, a mere glance at Job showed how wicked he was, and seven days and nights of watching his suffering could only deepen the impression that came when they had first heard that he had lost his property— that he must have been a very doubtful character, in spite of appearances, from the first. This was their theology. It was the test of their orthodoxy that they were on the side of the lost she-asses and the boils. They very truly said that they could not do differently — they and the Lord. It was the Mosaic conception of duty and its reward. Job was a most unquestionable heretic. He did not have a shadow of precedent in his favor. Seven deaths, and a missing fortune, the Sabeans and their swords, fire and wind, were their argument, and a wife, with her " Curse God and die." The real grandeur of Job was his impatience. His humility before God is but the more beautiful side of his anger with his friends, and his self-abasement before his Maker is the crowning dignity of a self-respect which is one of the epics of the world. The only proof he had of his righteousness was himself. And he bowed before his Maker and believed in Him because he dared to believe in that self against hail and fire and death and the words of men and the fear of their prim little dogma-god. " My righteousness I hold fast and will not let it go "— the parable of every hero ; wonderful now, but more wonderful then, when Job fought the mighty fight alone, and went before us all down through sorrow to the heart of God.

His maintaining his righteousness in the face of evil was the shadow of the Messiah. Christ did not argue about the cross. He died on it. The argument was in Job. Isaiah prophesied the glory of suffering—the suffering of the righteous; Job proved it in his life, Christ with his death. The whole Hebrew faith had been put into a honey-comb of special providences, and with all this array of disaster the friends of Job either had to give up Job's righteousness or God's; either believe that every detail of good and evil that happened to them was a special providence, which was religion; or special improvidence, which was atheism.

It was because Job would do neither that he struck out a new path and won the freedom of God — the right to bring evil upon those he loved; one of the first instances in the world in which breadth was more practical than narrowness. Job was the discoverer of a practical faith which would stand the test of life, because he was the first to take God's point of view — to see that in the nature of the case it must be a universe; that a God whose point of view was not the universe would not be a God at all.

Infinity was gained with its perspective. It was something more than an ornament of Deity—a poetic invocation. It was God himself living into a vast system in which every soul and sorrow and blessing had its place. The dovetailing of rewards into one little existence—the whole creation a body-servant for a worthy Jew—Job had the sublime humor of every greater poet, and the Little God who does little things for little men to gain a little faith for a little time, puttering with their egotism to win their souls, vanished. The egotism which is the religion of the little man when he succeeds, the infidelity of the little man when he fails, the " I," which is the essence of littleness, which is the blasphemy alike of creeds and curses and prayers and sneers, met its sublime, eternal, triumphant rebuke in Job.

Though living under a false astronomy, he had just that quality of selflessness in his worship which would have made him surmise that the universe was not made to revolve around the earth as a center, or especially arranged to furnish heat and starlight to the Land of Uz. Such a discovery on Job's part would have been but the astronomical form of his theology.

7*

With the star measurements to measure himself and suggest his immeasurable God, Job did not expect the universe to be preoccupied with his estate, and performed his duty without requiring it.

He was too spiritual to have a Land of Uz God, or a Job's God, or a Jews' God. With their tiny, compacted, Land of Uz faith, his friends gathered around him, and accused him of blasphemy because God was so much more of a God to him than to them; because he gave Him room and gave Him time — the prerogatives of a God; because he saw that even a God was not divine enough to have a thousand centers, or hinge infinity on Uz.

With a breadth of conception that made the Creator nearer as well as farther, Job found in the vast itself the homelikeness the infinite alone can afford for our struggling human faith; the peace that passeth all understanding — peace just because it passeth all understanding. Eliphaz had to understand. He could have but the peace that comes a little at a time, as understanding

comes, and that moves away when understanding goes. The Infinite is the only rest
the finite has. Job rested in it.

From the point of view of Eliphaz and
Zophar, infinity in a God was unpractical.
It was vague — the nebula of divinity. It
had nothing definite to grasp. The men of
Uz could not be governed by the aurora
borealis. In the burning of a city, the re-
course of Eliphaz was the Sodom hypothesis
— an hypothesis which, like all narrowness,
was very practical from one side, if, con-
sidering the sins of men, one ignored, on
the other, that the least a logical God
could do would be to burn the city over
every year. The doctrine of Eliphaz by its
irreverent definiteness was the greatest practical encouragement toward wickedness in
his day. A motive for righteousness which
required constant fires could hardly be practical in a world which could only be kept
burning part of the time. Only a broader
law applying before a fire as well as after,
would be worthy of a jurist, or a God.

Thousands of miles of telegraph would

have been scientific proof with which to balance the striking of his flocks by lightning; but Job was a poet. He could take for granted. Mystery was a conviction in his theology, and humbleness, and giving God the benefit of a doubt, and when the great wind smote his sons, he did not need several thousand years of windmills and the sails that discovered the New World, to be sure that God's arrangements were best, or sure that wind had suddenly become a personal affront, had come from the ends of the earth across snows and seas to rebuke a man named Job. Job was practical because he was broad. He had a definite solution for the struggle of life because he was vague. Mystery was the conviction that made his theology at once the sublimest and most practical conception of the living One.

He was the first to give God time, the first to give Him room, the first to see His long looks, His glances of a thousand years. Out of the treasuries of the snow, the guiding of mornings and wandering of nights, and all the vast and beautiful care of the infinite heart, Job learned the awe that was to make his faith one of the mighty memories of men.

Thus he was the emancipator of righteousness, the inspirer of pain. He shall be remembered as the redeemer of sorrow, one who could sing with a cross; one who lifted duty above reward and degraded sin below punishment, because he discovered the infinity of God, because he lost himself in the wideness of His ways.

XVII

Doth Not Wisdom Cry and Understanding Put Forth Her Voice?

SOLOMON could not keep the Proverbs. So he wrote them. The founder of moral philosophy — the duty which Moses stated and David attempted, Solomon explained. Morality passed into its motto stage.

But the prayer at the dedication of the temple must be read with the eleventh chapter of Kings.[1] And "Without me ye can do nothing."

A book with a less inspired conception than the Bible, of religion, and therefore of art, following the more common human instinct, would have suppressed this chapter in Kings. Solomon's literary executors,

[1] But King Solomon loved many strange women . . . and his wives turned away his heart.

seeing that it would jar upon the artistic unity of his work, would have arranged the writing of his biography with decorous deceit. It would have had all those un-prophetic omissions that belong to the narrower idea of beauty and the smaller artists' cowardice of life. The readers of Proverbs for thousands of years would have innocently longed to be like Solomon. The world would have been set back in its spiritual achievement for an indefinite period, and all those reserves of knowledge which come of knowledge experiencing itself, would have been lost. Confidently working upon the impossible, full of the glad consciousness that the Proverbs were the solution of moral effort; in the blind, crude ways of life would the world have learned that there had been a lie somewhere — a moral romance — that had to be suffered and suffered away from the human heart — because the perfect finish of Solomon's art had been preserved.

To the sublime literary morality of the Bible we are indebted for the fact that the most valuable contribution that Solomon made to us was not thus sacrificed — the comment of the eleventh chapter of Kings upon the three thousand Proverbs. Called the wisest man in the world because he repented in *bons mots*, because no one has had so gifted a repentance since, Solomon will be immortal in the minds of men, because of his consummate literary longing to have them do wrong more wisely. Eloquence is not having what we want, but wanting it. Wisdom is the art of demanding that others shall do better than ourselves. A proverb is saying what we wish we had done, or hoped that we would, and all the wise sayings that stretch their dainty rhetoric over our naked lives are the inventories of our ignorance — the retrospect of the beauty we have lost.

The great Redeemer Satire of the Old Testament, Solomon comes to us the climax of the bitter truth — the human heart waiting with words, bitterly with words — with words — outside of the gates of Bethlehem. Giving to the Hebrews a larger assortment of thoroughly understood sins, and no inspiration to avoid them, except an ironical life — " I have not kept these Proverbs; how much less chance there is for you, who cannot even say them "—this was the mission of the wisest man in the world.

And yet that it was better for men to do wrong intelligently than ignorantly, this passing phase of mottoes shall stand as one of the records of God. The moral philosophy which had been simply God's convenience, came to an end in this questioning and observing of life. Solomon went back of the divine will to the nature of things. Bringing the Law out from the mere authority of One in whom a man might believe or might not, he surrounded it with the authority of this actual world, in which a man has to live, whatever he believes. It was the discovery of reasonableness, of what might be called the mind of God.

The natural rudimentary Mosaic attitude toward a fire — not that it blisters, but that

it has been said, " Thou shalt not touch it,"
— finds its supplement in Solomon; and the
higher obedience, based upon knowledge, in
the brilliant son of David comes to its first
great emphasis. Philosophy was the study
of blisters.

Discovering a larger man, as Job had discovered a larger God, he represents a hu-
manist movement, the turning of man to
himself — the self-discovery which wrought
out as a habit of thought the identity of
the moral law with the nature of man. A
teacher of the experiences of morality, Solomon connected the mystical voice of Sinai
with the conscience of every day, and the religion of what they knew about themselves
as well as the religion of what they had been
told about their God was given to the race.

But the higher value of Solomon's reign
was not this. It is only by standing in
the ruins of his temple that we can worship
there, can read in the mighty, broken outlines the truth at last. Built with proverb
and stone and gold, it is one of the great
half-truths of history, completed alone by

being half destroyed. The Saracen in fierce
unconsciousness was to become the interpreter of Solomon, bringing to its logical
conclusion in the dust of the earth the gospel of the eleventh chapter of Kings.

At once the discoverer of moral philosophy as the theory of heaven and the way
to hell, Solomon is the immortal illustration
of the merely moral man — not that he was
moral, or that the merely moral man is ever
moral, but that he is impossible. The oft-
recurring type of the broad and understanding man who enlarges the area of the
truth without having life enough to cover
it, finds its great original in one who sub-
stituted reasonableness for righteousness
and forgot God in building a temple for
Him.

The history of the human race is the
Brobdingnag biography of every unknown
soul. The passing phases of our lives are
the old shadows of these mightier destinies
that have crossed our world, to prove with a
classic tragedy what we know with a passing thought.

Nations have been born and lived and died to furnish the moral philosophy of a child, of an afternoon. With a thousand years and a million sorrowing hearts tucked into his epigrams, Solomon himself shall be to us an unforgotten proverb — a great experience of the world. Writing a book which has the distinction of being the only book in the Bible that every one outgrows, his appeal is to the time of crudeness, when observation is still piety and the will not yet unmasked, still proud of its trim omnipotence. In the time of spiritual glibness and dogmatic confidence, in the zest of our ignorance, we conjure inspiration out of Proverbs and dream of life, but to life itself must always come the wondering humbleness of the New Testament. To live is yet to look back upon Solomon's sayings with sad wonder at ourselves. With their tiny courtly glory in the struggle of the years, they but linger by the name of Christ — dim, pathetic decorations on the sternness and the realness and the silence of the cross.

David was not a philosopher, and Solomon would have patronized the childishness of his father's faith, but the Son of God was called the son of David because Solomon was not; and the only value of the temple that the wise king built, was that his father's prayers would be prayed there, that long after the stately obviousness of the Proverbs had become an old ornament in the world, the songs of David's spirit should be upon the lips of the nations as far as sin and longing and hope and fear have reached their cries upon the earth—the wise earth—the wearily-wise earth—the hungering and thirsting earth—parched with proverbs—dying with epigrams—waiting for God.

XVIII

Vanity! Vanity! All is Vanity

ECCLESIASTES is the text-book of suicides.
Though not without hope, the hope is a
gilded discouragement, lighting the world
to show how dark it is. Only in a book
as supremely victorious as the Bible could
such an appealing and beautiful prophecy of
despair be safely printed. It is the shadow-
song of the earth. It is the masterpiece of
the Night. It is the culmination of the
Proverbs and the lives of the kings. "As
when a hungry man dreameth and behold
he eateth, and he waketh and his soul
is empty." Sadder than David's Psalms,
because they had tears; sadder than death,
because there was no death, it is the confes-
sional of wisdom, and through its wonderful lines, hallowed with a broken heart, the

restless spirit of man shall move forever to
find in its forbidding fellowship, its sublime
self-pity, the *Miserere* of the world.   Even
when the poet comes to his climax and
struggles toward joy — "Rejoice, O young
man.   Remove sorrow from thine heart,"—
the *Gloria* strives for its voices in the song of
youth only to modulate into death, death,
death, "When the mourners go about the
streets and the dust returns to the earth as
it was and the spirit to God who gave it."
"Vanity! Vanity! All is vanity!"— the
litany of philosophy, closing at last with its
saddest sentence, "All hath been heard,"
in the middle of the Bible.

The pitiful attempt at a New Testament,
Ecclesiastes is the caricature of a Proverb
straining to be a cross. The immortal argument of the merely moral man confuted by
himself, it marks at once the beginning of
moral philosophy as a contribution to man-
kind, and the end of moral philosophy as
the solution of human life.

The author of Ecclesiastes, whoever he
may have been, was a man like men : a uni-

versal man. The last testament of a man
of affairs — a scholar, a seer, a diplomat, a
lover,— it cannot be set aside as the dis-
couraged wisdom of a monk or the pessim-
ism of an aloof life.

> I adjure you, O daughters of Jerusalem,
> By the roes and the hinds of the fields,
> That ye stir not up nor waken love

— the wooing strain in the song of Solomon floats softly through all the lines of
what must ever stand as the most experienced book in the Old Testament; the very
force and completeness of which is alto-
gether lost if it is not the symphony of a
wonderful and various life. The love-song
motif, "Awake, O North Wind, and blow
thou South!" like the ghost of a brighter
melody through the mighty minor chords
that sing the weariness of the world, winds
ever like a beauty that is lost, not by being
overlooked, but by having been lived down
through to bitterness. "One generation
goeth and another generation cometh, and

the earth abideth forever," and the minor
chords, and "That which hath been is that
which shall be, and that which is to be hath
already been, and God seeketh again that
which hath passed away."

"All hath been heard." The voices are
still and the world sleeps and dreams and
waits. The hush of darkness is upon it. It
is the starlight Revelation.

No man knoweth. The morning comes
at midnight—only to God.

XIX

The Shadow Christ

I

IT was a most startling hypothesis that came to the unknown Isaiah: "If God were to come to Judea and live, what kind of man would he be?"

To be original is to discover the commonplace of a thousand years — to face at first the sneer that no one would have thought of it, and at last the indifference because any one would. He who thinks a mighty thought weaves him an immortal shroud. Fame is the beginning of forgetting. To be great is to take one of the habits of the gods—to move everywhere unknown — to be accorded the world for a burial-ground — to be a spirit, a thought — to breathe through the unnamed winds. To be great is to be capable of becoming

as commonplace as the rustling of the
leaves, and sunshine, and Christ. It shall
need a prophet to tell who a prophet was
— to distill his spirit out of the souls of men.
He shall be a wraith, gathered out of life
like the morning mists. Men shall strive
to divine his face, shall paint and sing
— shall seek to say, "This is he"; but out
of the Dust and the Spirit he came. To
the Spirit and the Dust he shall return.

Immortality has been the romance of
little men thrumming their harps in a little
age. Out of the ground itself has science
brought its mighty measure. It shall be
a silent word. With his tinsel little thousands of years, there is one who sings the
loves of a woman in Troy. His name is
called immortal. With the pantomime of
history flocking through his heart, there is
one who sings the coming of the love of
God, and the generations ask, "What is
his name? Where was his abiding-place?
Who knew him first?" And the answer
shall be to every man: "His name shall
be upon thy forehead. The spirit in thine

eyes shall be to him for a name. Its secret shall be life."

A prophet shall be the world itself. His
breath shall blow from the seas. His immortality shall be nameless—like the im-
mortalities of God—through the passing
of flowers and suns. He shall be a conviction. He shall be a habit among the sons
of men. About his spirit we shall build the
faint and curious scaffoldings of history—
that we may strive to rebuild his life. We
shall gather from afar the tokens of his time
— the pathetic little heaps—the dust of
research. We shall blow it wisely in each
other's eyes; but we shall not know—that
greatest knowledge of all—that knowledge
of how knowledge came—that knowledge
of how it was before the knowledge came;
or guess but dimly that mighty day when
the Incarnation Truth was fresh in the heart
of a man—fresh as the face of the earth
when God gazed down that Creation morning, when He unfolded it out of darkness
and loved it first.

We shall never know how dark it was nor

how light the light was, when, like a vast
conjecture—amorphous, terrible, beautiful,
tender, infinite, in the spirit of one who
dreamed, there loomed the great Redeemer-
Dream and sounded the chorus of all the
earth—when to the first disciple of Jesus,
hundreds of years away, there came as
generations coming with oratorios on their
lips:

Hast thou not known? Hast thou not heard?
Hath it not been told thee from the beginning?

It is the everlasting God — the Lord — the
Creator of the ends of the earth —

then the sudden silence—the Isaiah silence
—and the sweetest, strangest solo in all the
world singing like a little child's heart:

He shall feed His flock like a shepherd; He
shall gather the lambs in His arms and carry
them in His bosom, and gently lead those that
are with young.

The time of the blending of a human
song with the music of the spheres, when

Isaiah caught the longing of God from the
stars — when he knew the divinity of His
coming down — bitterly and completely
down — to the love of Mary and the cry
on the Cross.

The more beautiful Bethlehem was in
Isaiah's heart. Like the Wise Men of the
East, Moses and Job and David had brought
their offerings there, and in the synthesis
of the three great conceptions of God — in
the wonder of their being together — the
book that is called Isaiah is the struggle of
the world's dream — the Saviour sleep — the
unwaked New Testament.

XX

The Shadow Christ

II

A GREAT man is one who makes the world greater to find room for himself. A thousand years to him and God are but as yesterday when it is passed. He has the mimic omnipresence of a soul wont to walk under the eaves of heaven with the Maker of the earth. The mighty one of every era is thousands of years away from those who dwell with him, and all the great men of the scattered years are nearer to each other than to the dates that gossip on their tombstones —the little difference that it makes when they are born, or the figures that tell us when they could not die.

The hero's solitude is his fellowship with heroes. From the years to the east and the years to the west they come. The paths

are short between the centuries, when,
seeking their mighty kindred, the great go
forth to visit in a prophet's heart; and from
the beginning of the world transfiguration
is the habit, the secret of every colossal
life. "Live, O my mighty brother," the
Secret says, "live in the littleness about
thee, doomed to the dullness, gentle with
the pain. When the empty roar is stilled
and over the dear blind makers of the Noise
shall reach the great soft hand of Sleep—
there shall be the sound of coming—the
gathering of thy brothers from afar; in the
peace above the world shalt thou walk
with them. In the trysting-place of prophets thou shalt touch their hands. From
their eyes thy soul shall drink. As the
night gathers the dew, their thought shall
descend upon thee—glistening, refreshing,
full of morning love; it shall be to thee
for solemn delight—the faith for thy sacrifice. It shall be the word thou shalt
speak when the Dawn and thou go down
between the hills. Thou shalt not look
back nor falter. Thy brotherhood with

prophets shall be to live without them. It shall be to believe in the greatness of little men—calling to it—pleading with it. Whether it come to thy face or to thy cross or to thy grave, their greatness shall be for thy greatness—created out of thy heart, humbled with thy sorrow, builded into the world."

The "Comfort ye, comfort ye, my people" was the Unknown Isaiah's way of coming down from transfiguration.

Going to and fro, looking into every face for a hero, demanding, expecting, challenging, believing, Isaiah prophesied the Christ. Across the souls of his brothers he saw Him coming. Out of the east, out of the west, out of the north and the south, out of sorrow and exile and desire and despair—the gathering of God—to be born in Bethlehem. The Wise Men saw the star in the East and came across the deserts to the birth. Isaiah saw it in the spirit of men. He was in Gethsemane. The cry of the mob and the cry on the cross were convictions in the struggle of his life. His prophecy was the irrevocable insight of love. The Night gathered as he gazed upon men. Tenderly and softly over his glowing thoughts, the Christ-spirit came—the hush, the Shadow, the Cross. It was no fragmentary, unconnected, beautiful reverie of sadness, coming like a voice on the air to be noted down with a pen. It was not a reported prophecy. It was life itself. It was his coming down from a transfiguration, it was the more actual, intimate prophecy—written on the street. Looking into his brothers' eyes he wrote it. He saw that the denials of Peter were there, that the stripes of Pilate could not be helped, and that Philip's cruel question was eternal upon the lips of men. He knew. He utterly knew—that on an earth where even a man could not be great without a sorrow, a God without a cross would not even be a man.

It was no great outside angel's voice leaning over his trembling body and telling him to write. It was no journalistic divining of events, no inspired information

of circumstance. It was a profound experience with the nature and law of life — a
colossal judgment of the human race. ·

Gazing into its grandeur and its cowardice, he saw the inevitable conflict there.
Out of the human heart itself deciphered
the Creator's Secret for this earth — the
passion of history — the Gethsemane — the
Truth.

XXI

The Shadow Christ

III

ISAIAH'S transfiguration — his talking with Jesus across the generations — his outreaching through the future for a Man, was but the half of his prophecy. There have been candidates for prophets and candidates for saviours. There have been great-men-elect — natures that have conquered the forty days' fast and the temptation with Satan — who could not put their transfigurations behind them — and failed. Poets may live in transfigurations. Prophets will not. They may go there to rest — as Christ with Moses and Elias — to be soothed a little, to feel the coolness and the peace of God's hand, that it may touch for a moment the fever on their brows. Then to work.

The mingling of a transfiguration and a

fact makes a prophet possible. The looking for a Man *now* makes him inevitable.
Poetry may be truth. Prophecy is where
truth connects with the next thing to do.
It is the sad end of the truth, but it is the
end where heroes are, where ideals are ideal-
ized into facts, where great men, struggling
for their faith, reach up their holy hands as
though they would fasten the skies to the
earth, as though with their very crosses they
would hold them low for the prayers of men.
The forgetful transfiguration may be more
beautiful than the applied one—the foreign
beauty, the unrighteous beauty of peace
when there is no peace; but Isaiah prophesied the incarnation because incarnation
was the habit of his life. He speaks the
truth for all times because he was trying
to find a truth big enough for his own—
and build it there. This is the essential
fact about the essential prophecy of history. It was incarnation that conceived
Incarnation.

The bare idea of having a Messiah turns
upon the Isaiah experience without one—

9

the fierce intentness of a practical struggler
with a nation, forced into prophecy by the
problem of life — the problem that comes
to all of us, as, out of the sad and scattered years, comrades of the sun and comrades of the grave, we walk between them,
this one great question ringing in our ears
through the irrevocable days: "Shall we
be impossible gods, poor wistful gods, half-
created gods, on this earth of men; or shall
we not?"—the challenge of the incarnation.
To accept it is to live with the divine, the infinite, the unattainable, striking its splendid sorrow through all our deeds — beautiful, incomplete, glorious, defeated, dying.
To refuse it is to mumble a love of what
we dare not be, and call it worship. It is
to whimper for a better world and call it
religion. It is to be abdicated gods, because divinity has no chance withal, because
there are no conveniences for heroes on the
earth.

When our hearts are in tumult, and we
are cast down, the incarnation challenge
comes. When the day is over, when our

brother has returned us hate for love, dullness for insight, when he has cursed the
dearest we could give, we shall go forth
to the calm and absent-looking sky.   We
shall say: "It were simple to be a God —
safe beyond the stars."   From the vast
resting-places in the deep the winds shall
come to us.   They shall blow upon the
fever in our faces and we shall say: "It
were simple enough to be a God — off
where the winds begin; to be a God alone,
to be a monk-God, with a universe for a
hermitage, with worlds for infinite retreat;
but to be a god *here*, to have a god's
desires and a man's chance — to be mock-
ingly eternal and cabined in days and
nights,— to be infinite and dream stars, and
be riveted down to the ground,— to have
wings of love and be fastened to hate and
wedded to blindness and mingled with
beasts and harried hither and thither in the
great unseemly shambles, where men think
they live and do not even learn to die, and
where they curse, and cast their souls into
the filth, and trample their brothers under

their feet for the filth itself, and burn their heroes at the stake! Safe in infinity, with all Space in which to be Himself, shall a God who has made the worlds as He wished them to be require a man to be a god in a world which he did not make, a world which he did not choose, a world where to undertake to be a *man* is more than a god would care to do?" Thus the incarnation challenge comes,

It were indeed a god's world, framed for heaven, with its vast delights, bounded by skies and singing its own music day unto day. With one's own soul listening in it, it were easy to be a god alone—to let the links of light and the links of darkness, of song and starlight and sleep, fall across the years and bind us to its joy forever. It were easy to be a god thus—or to be a god with gods,—to troop through the vales of the earth and look into each other's souls; but to be a god with *men?*

The problem of every soul when the sons of God go forth to live.

Therefore God's problem—the struggle

with environment. The Messianic answer was the conviction of history, the gathered voice of the human race, exalted into the utterance of one who prophesied the Messiah because to him a God who would ask of His creatures more than He would do Himself would not be a God at all.

Thus came to pass the tremulous gospel —the writing of John across the soul of Isaiah.

"In the beginning was the Word and the Word was with God and the Word was God and the Word was made flesh and dwelt among men."

XXII

The Shadow Christ

IV

THE righteousness of God had been conceived before. Moses had bound it about
the soul. His fatherhood had been conceived. David had sung it into one of
the habits of Hebrew life. Job had made
it an infinite fatherhood. Ethics had been
thought out as a science. Men had conceived of a man in God's place for thousands of years. The man had been their
God. Isaiah was a poet and conceived of
a God in a man's place. The turning of
this thought was the crisis of the world.
Henceforth worship, which had been an
effort—a scattering, an outgoing of the
human heart into the Vast, a spreading of
our little prayers across the sky—should
be an incoming, a shining down. The in-

carnation was the concentration of God—
the decree that the infinite should be the
neighborhood of life.

But the greater idea, in its divine necessity, its logicalness, was not Isaiah's idea
of having a Messiah. It was his idea of
what He would be when He came: the incredible conception that when the Maker
of the earth descended, He would be de-
spised and rejected of men—the sublimest
accusation of history, the supreme satire
upon the human race, the most beautiful
and awful reach of insight the world has
known.

It was the intense humanness of this
divinest prophet which alone could have
anticipated the divinity, not of God's being
a God, but the greater divinity of His being
a man; His giving up a God's opportuni-
ties, His being a struggling God, with the
little human outfit of Space and Time and
Circumstance with which He asked Isaiah
to be a prophet for Him and Peter to die
for Him.   There came to the vision of the
seer, the Cross — the Consistent Creator—

showing to the human heart what He really was. Approaching his conception out of the atmosphere of the God of Israel instead of the memory of the Saviour Himself, Isaiah's anticipation bears within it a sense of the divine sacrifice so profound, so masterful, so full of praise and onwardness, of vast, exultant sorrow, that it sweeps its glorious tides into the New Testament itself, where the soul of Isaiah overflows and breaks its prophecies upon the words of Paul and fills the very presence of Christ with the fullness of the past.

It is too much to expect that a man great enough to prophesy a Messiah should have been at hand to interpret him when He came, but one cannot but wonder how much more the gospel of Luke would have revealed of the soul of Christ if it had been written by one who understood Jesus without seeing Him, instead of one who did not understand Him when he did; and while the cruelty of the love that was offered Christ was the supreme necessity of an honest incarnation, one cannot but wonder

whether "the things I have yet to say unto
you, but ye cannot bear them now," would
not have been spoken, if there had been one
great heroic soul endowed with habits and
insights that would comprehend — to stand
between this farewell talk, this pitiful re-
serve of Jesus and the human heart.

But the sound of the truth shall not be
lost. It matters not. With the tide and
the sun God brings it back. If the great
listener be not at hand, his soul shall gather
the murmur out of the ages as the shell
gathers the sea. Luther takes the keys
out of Peter's hands and Isaiah hears the
Beatitudes in his grave,— one before whose
father-messiah spirit the blundering pea-
sants who walked with Jesus shall be as children forever, before whose majestic vision
the inspired insight of the great apostle to
the Gentiles becomes but the beautiful
makeshift of the day, in the crisis of the
kingdom on the earth.

Does no one feel the dim stirring, the
sense of what it would have been, if but
one of Paul's epistles could have been as-

signed to Isaiah—if he who wrote the mighty fore-word had left but one gentle retrospect—if he who spoke the sublimely unfulfilled had sung the fulfillment itself? We may go, it is true, through all history with our wistful "might have beens." All is answered and answered once for all, by the divine *was*. We may dare to reconstruct the past, because it is safe from our petty hands; but to ask what Paul would have written had he been in Isaiah's place? Conjecture is the huge shadow-measurement of men. Against its flickering outlines we may lift a soul and trace its greatness on the lives of heroes and the thoughts of God. Would Paul have prophesied the Christ—barely convinced by the Christ Himself? Would he have written anything at all, in that hopelessness which was Isaiah's opportunity? Paul was one who held garments while Isaiahs were being stoned. He belonged to the second order of great men—those who see afterward. The supreme great man of the divine visit to the earth, wrapped in his thousand years, side

by side with Peter, who knew him yesterday, Isaiah walks. Through his radiant
New Testament soul, past the metaphysics
of Paul and the letters of John the hearts
of men gaze deep to know what their
Messiah was.

From the point of view of a God de-
scending to live with men—Isaiah's point
of view—the emphasis that has been placed
upon the cross, the more glaring, obvious
cross, must have been the hardest part of
dying on it. The picturesqueness—the
vulgar appeal of the subtlest, divinest, si-
lentest, most ceaseless sorrow on the earth
—the cross was the narrowing down of the
incarnation, not to its consummate point,
but to its final inexpressibleness. It was
the final attempt to crowd the infinite love
which had been manifested more in the
patience and divineness of every day, into
the tiny, awful word that men call *Death*
—the shallow side of suffering.

Standing in the awful light of that moment when Jesus died for them—so much
more awful to them than to Him—so much

more awful than it was to them when they died themselves—the simple and terrified hearts of the Apostles wrote their memories of the Christ. They could not but be morbid with the cross. It was the key-moment through which they came to all the other moments, and through its immeasurable rebuke they wrote the life and interpreted the days that had passed. But Isaiah's insight did not come through the blinding misery of his own cowardice and the forsaken death of God. He saw Him through the stern exigencies of his own prophetic life—the greater, more sympathetic, more kindred way of seeing Him—the way that men who see before instead of afterward must always see. He saw what He had given up. He saw Him coming from infinite opportunity to crowd a god into a man as *he* was trying to crowd a prophet into a man. He knew the dread necessities He had taken upon his soul as one to whom the real cross would be not dying before—would be coming here at all—an insight which makes the fortieth and fifty-

third of Isaiah the supreme interpretation
of the New Testament, though a solitary
soul was singing it hundreds of years away.

To play at being men like the gods of
the Greeks, to play at being gods like the
poets and the dreamers of the earth, were
not difficult; but to be in grim earnest, with
uttermost faithfulness, a half-god, with a
god's ideals and a man's body in a man's
world; to be a half-man with a god's desires—Incarnation is the eternal essence
of sorrow—the great creative sorrow which
has been the dignity and the destiny of
the strong from the beginning of the world.
From the Incarnation downward, which
was the story of Christ, to the Incarnation
upward, which is the history of the human
race, Savonarola and God by the birth in
Bethlehem are brought into the same great
tragedy—the manhood of the one, "I will
be God"; the divinity of the other, "I
will be a man." The great man's conception of a great Messiah, a conception which,
approaching the divine life from the God's
point of view, makes the manger in the inn

a mightier fact than the Cross, and Christ-
mas the anniversary of the greatest sorrow
in the world.

By a natural process in the endeavor to
reach the feelings of the coarsest men, we
have come to emphasize the very release
of Jesus as His crowning sacrifice, because
it took a form which the very brutes of
the field would have dimly understood, and
had the impressiveness of the fundamental
awe of human life on which to move. The
result is an exaggerated, lurid cross, loom-
ing high in the consciousness of men,
because it is nearest to them, because death
is the nearest word to terror, the shibbo-
leth of cowards, of those who have lived
not yet where life is deep enough to feel
the gentleness of a grave, or know the way
it greets a hero, or folds its rest about the
incarnation-ones who suffer out the destinies of men.

The prayer in the later days, "Thy will
and not mine be done," shall not be nar-
rowed down to the fear of suffering. It
shall be widened out into the hope of suf-

fering longer, the insistence of the incarnation, the spirit of One who in His conflict would have died on three crosses for three more years—of love and tireless trust and infinite expectancy—One who knew that He must die to prove to the world who He was, but who could not believe—not yet, not quite yet—"Oh, my Father, if it be possible let this cup pass from me!"—that He must die to prove to Peter and James and Philip who He was. To prove ourselves to those who hate, by dying—that might be—but to prove ourselves to those who love, to have them side by side wayfaring with us—dear outsiders in our hearts—to unfold our very souls to them—and ask, "Hast thou been so long time with me and dost thou not know me?"—to draw their faces in vain to our faces—to know that they will come at last, that they will look down into the eternal silence there—that they will love too late. This is Gethsemane love. To pass on with an incarnation that has failed—to serve our brothers by being remembered instead of joining our hands with their hands and giving them our very selves—to give up the privilege of dying every day and die once—this was the cross of One who hoped to the last to found His kingdom upon the recognition of men instead of their infinite penitence. The hero, be he man or God, chooses the living death. He will live in sorrows that make the grave beautiful—a paradise of dust. He will live to sorrow out service for men who make the grave terrible only because it has no more to give, because there shall be no reaching out there, and no cry shall be heard there, and we are drawn into the dumbness of the earth.

The conception which for hundreds of years in the Church—in the counting off of souls and the worship of results—has made the fear of death the courage for conversion, finds but a refinement of itself in the emphasis of the cross—an emphasis which, while it is perfectly just and true and Messianic without the remotest question, is open to the objection that it is not

Messianic enough, that it is based on an essential under-estimate of One who was crucified first with the love that was borne Him, then with the hate—who died between two thieves—forever the symbols of His being on the earth, of the strange, sweet, triumphant fellowship He took upon Himself—a fellowship which above and beyond the cross, every day and every hour of misunderstanding, was itself the faithfulness, the realness, the bitter literalness of the incarnation—the being a God —a Comrade-God, among the sons of men.

The Shadow Christ

V

THE talking of Jesus with Moses and Elias
is the secret way back to Isaiah's prophecy
for the modern heart — the parable of
Isaiah's life.

Born with the instincts of greatness, one
of the kindred of heroic vision, Elias was
not as far from Jesus as the way Peter and
James and John looked, when they were
told what the Kingdom really was. They
stand as the sorrowful symbol of contemporary faith in every age, toward every
prophet. Wistful, wondering, struggling,
ordinary men, day after day, in attracted
dullness, they had hung upon His words.
In the only way in which men who were
arguing who should be greatest could call
Him out, they called Him out; but there

came a time when there was nothing for
them to do but to stand apart — to watch
their Master talking with the great.

To Peter and James and John the transfiguration was the way Jesus had never
looked for them — the shining in His face
when great hearts loved Him back — the
moment of His being understood.

To Jesus it was the moment of the
mighty listeners, the moment when the
men He might have had and the men He
had to have faced each other — when the
heartache of the difference shot its pain
through the shining in His face.

In the soul of the Saviour they stood,
these two groups of love. Between them
a Cross. A transfiguration with Peter and
James and John shut out, an absent-minded
transfiguration, could not have come to
Him. He was too great for that. He could
face His fact and His faith in the one same
calm, beautiful mood. It was the very essence
of His greatness to think of the fishermen
then. The one moment of utter brotherhood in His pitilessly solitary life, with the

neighbors of His spirit by His side—He was a Saviour because it was but a moment. He gave the password of the great, and then walked down the mountain to love ordinary James and try again with Judas and be Peter's brother until He died. The more beautiful transfiguration was the one on the way down, when, listening to the prattle of His apostles, transfiguration became incarnation. "Here in this little Galilee, *here*, *now*, with this self-same Peter, with this poor, pitiful James—HERE, NOW, I WILL BE THE SON OF GOD!"

Out of the struggle between his transfiguration love and his love of men, Isaiah prophesied an incarnation like this—mighty, daily, irrevocable, immeasurable—the unceasing crucifixion of the Christ. The incarnation was the expectancy of God—His trusting the human heart even beyond a cross,—even unto living with it. It was only an expectant Isaiah, expectant enough to incarnate, who could have prophesied an expectant Messiah, expectant enough to be a comrade with Judas and

Pilate and Mary Magdalene. Incarnation is the literalness of expectancy — the very experiencing of it. The " shall " which is but the room the prophet invokes from the greatness of God, out of centuries and nations, to fulfil himself, was but Isaiah's indomitable NOW, thrown into the long lenses, magnified by the spirit, stretched upon the years. The slide of one intense experience casts the outlines and colors of his soul upon the largest canvas of God. He is the portrait of an age — a prophet. Peter might have read the history of eighteen hundred years in the Saviour's eyes, had he been a prophet, and Isaiah's face was the shadowing of Christ's.

In the human stress, the agony of solitude, the vow of his own creative love, Isaiah lifted his heart to the ideal. " Not by being great thyself — not by needing great men around thee — but by making great men out of those thou hast, shalt thou be mine," saith the Lord. " In mine own godlike handiwork shalt thou come to me. Men thou shalt bring, wouldst thou be a man."

This was the Isaiah spirit. Striving to connect his transfiguration, struggling to say NOW, he discovered the Man of Sorrows and acquainted with grief.

Wrought out of stolid human heart by the slowly coming Christ, Isaiah was the first great miracle of His spirit. He prophesied the Messiah He had tried to be. Lifted into the shadow of the mighty love, he was the Almost Christ, the Christ of the Night.

"Not having received the promises, but having seen them and greeted them from afar."

"Having confessed that they were strangers and pilgrims on the earth, that they were seeking a country of their own."

www.ingramcontent.com/pod-product-compliance
Lightning Source LLC
Chambersburg PA
CBHW021109020726
47500CB00003B/670